What readers are saying about *Ship It!*

This is fantastic stuff. As I started reading, I almost fell out of my seat because the project I'm on right now is going through *exactly* the hurt you describe and would benefit greatly from material just like this.

▶ **Matthew Bass**
Software Engineer

Much like the Mac, this book "just works", because it takes the best from lessons learned from team leaders and team players and takes the mystery out of the project management processes as applied to Software Development... *Ship It!* is a surprisingly quick read and if you are in the software development food chain, this book pays for itself in a matter of hours.

▶ **Robert Pritchett**
macCompanion

It would be really nice if, as an industry, we could stop being such a bunch of screwed-up clowns and start living up to our potential. *Ship It!* is one of the things that could help, if only those who need the advice in its covers would pay attention.

▶ **Mike Gunderloy**
Larkware

It's a special feeling when you give someone a book and it changes the way they think and act. So I'm really pleased to have just finished reading a book that I know I'll be handing out time and time again, and that's *Ship It!*

▶ **Jeffery Fredrick**
CruiseControl

It's a rare book that speaks convincingly to both developers and managers, but this one does a good job.... My favorite part of the book is the compendium of one-page essays on common problems software projects have, and how to apply the principles and practices from the book to solve them. Unlike some other rather strained "antipatterns" catalogs that I've read, this section feels very practical and usable.

▶ **Ernest Friedman-Hill**
Java Ranch

A great book! The authors have done a great job in presenting the subject in a neutral way and avoiding any methodology-oriented traps.

▶ **Roberto Gianassi**
IT Consultant

What *The Pragmatic Programmer* brought to the individual skills and crafts of software developers, *Ship It!* is to the software development team. If you or someone you know in the software field isn't happy, then get them to read this book.

▶ **Guerry A. Semones**
Senior Software Engineer, Appistry

It's rare to have this much fun reading a book about software. The ideas are smart, relevant, and fundamental. I can be a better programmer *today* because of the things I read *today*.

▶ **Joe Fair**

Ship It! is in the style of the other Pragmatic books and is an easy and focused read. I finished it in two days and have already gained a wealth of insight that I can apply immediately. Highly recommended if you want to streamline your software development life!

▶ **Anil John**

If you are a Development Team Lead or a Development Manager, you should be fired if you don't read this book.

▶ **David Starr**
Elegant Code

Ship It!

A Practical Guide to
Successful Software Projects

Ship It!

A Practical Guide to
Successful Software Projects

Jared R. Richardson

William A. Gwaltney Jr.

The Pragmatic Bookshelf

Raleigh, North Carolina   Dallas, Texas

Many of the designations used by manufacturers and sellers to distinguish their products are claimed as trademarks. Where those designations appear in this book, and The Pragmatic Programmers, LLC was aware of a trademark claim, the designations have been printed in initial capital letters or in all capitals. The Pragmatic Starter Kit, The Pragmatic Programmer, Pragmatic Programming, Pragmatic Bookshelf and the linking *g* device are trademarks of The Pragmatic Programmers, LLC.

Every precaution was taken in the preparation of this book. However, the publisher assumes no responsibility for errors or omissions, or for damages that may result from the use of information (including program listings) contained herein.

Our Pragmatic courses, workshops, and other products can help you and your team create better software and have more fun. For more information, as well as the latest Pragmatic titles, please visit us at

        http://www.pragmaticprogrammer.com

ISBN 0-9745140-4-7

Printed on acid-free paper with 85% recycled, 30% post-consumer content.

Third printing, August 2006

Version: 2006-7-6

Contents

Dogma does not mean the absence of thought, but the end of thought.

▶ Gilbert Keith Chesterton (1874–1936)

Foreword

You may have noticed that this isn't the only book about developing software sitting on the shelf.

In fact, not only are there a *lot* of books about designing and building software but they tend to disagree with one another. Unfortunately, these disagreements in approach usually generate more heat than light: as practitioners, we end up feeling burned, not enlightened. Oh, and the project we're working on still ends up late.

We continue to search for a better way of developing software (a method) that will work for us and our teams. But discussions of the benefits and drawbacks of various development methods tend to devolve into shouting matches, based chiefly on established dogma. The dictionary describes *dogma* as expressing a point of view put forth as authoritative but without adequate grounds. We see it all the time from proponents of various methods who insist that their approach is the only right way to develop software. We hear it constantly from practitioners who insist on doing things a certain way, even when it becomes demonstrably harmful to the rest of the team or the organization.

The fact is that there is no "right way" to develop software. There are a lot of wrong ways, but there's no single method, approach, philosophy, or tool that will work in all circumstances for all projects for all people all the time. Software is created by people, and no two people are alike.

So we try to remain pragmatic about our software development practices. We try to focus on the goal: do we really want a collection of signatures, or do we want everyone to understand? Do we want to fling a pile of bits over the wall on an arbitrary date or produce software that helps someone do their job?

We're willing to try new things and to constantly evaluate and revise our practices; we want to find what works *for us*. But it takes a lot of work to get started; it takes a lot of research and a lot of time—time that most working programmers don't have.

This brings me to the topic of Jared and Will's book. This book is a quick-start guide to basic, effective tools and techniques needed to get you producing reliable code regularly.

Jared and Will were among the first to read our book *The Pragmatic Programmer*, and they took its lessons to heart. They used our approach and techniques, along with practices from popular agile methodologies, and forged a method that has worked for them from small startups to the largest privately held software company in the world.

They've written up their favored techniques and practices in this book. You can jump-start your efforts at improving your development process with this information, perhaps augmented with some technical detail from the Pragmatic Starter Kit series. As time goes on, you may want to extend your reach and experiment with other practices and techniques. After all, that's the pragmatic way—finding what works best for you, today.

I hope you find this book helpful and that it takes you to the point where you can just sit back, relax, and tell the system to *Ship It!*

Andy Hunt, The Pragmatic Programmers, LLC
April 2005
andy@pragmaticprogrammer.com

Preface

One of the smartest investments you can make in yourself and your career is to surround yourself with the right people—they are the finest resource you'll ever find. These are the people who are already doing what you want to be doing, or what you want to learn to do. Find those people who can do exactly what you want to do, or at least find the really smart people who can figure out how to do anything. Spend as much time around them as you can. Learn from them by helping them and getting them to help you. Spending time with people of this caliber helps you learn and become better at your job (no matter what your job is).

This is a great idea, but getting direct access to the very best of the best and brightest can be difficult. People such as Martin Fowler, Kent Beck, and the Pragmatic Programmers are not available to most of us, but their books, articles, and presentations are. So start reading books. One a month shouldn't be too painful. But don't stop there; learn a new programming language, or study a different development process. And while you are learning and reading, find ways to apply these new ideas to your current work. Bring in new ideas to your day job. In doing so you will not only help improve your company but you will also (more importantly) improve yourself.

Expose yourself to new ideas. Rack your brain to find ways to apply these new ideas to your existing work. It is easier to give up and say that a new idea does not apply, but the goal is to learn to think in a different way. Live outside the box (or at least build a bigger box). Learn to overlay seemingly unrelated concepts and ideas.

By analyzing and critiquing your environment and process, you will find the weak spots. Maybe you will help make improvements on this project, or perhaps the next. But you will have practiced a new way of thinking that will serve you well no matter where you work. Most people never learn this concept, and fewer still become good at it.

So, as you finish each section of the book, stop and spend five minutes trying to find ways to use each concept for what you are doing today. Remember, the easiest answer, which requires no thought, is to say it cannot be done. Work harder than that! If you cannot find a way to apply the concept, grab a colleague and ask them. If you cannot see it through your own eyes, look though somebody else's. Knowing how to leverage co-worker's experience is a hallmark of a journeyman in any field.

Take what you read in this book (and the entire Pragmatic Starter Kit), and find a way to apply every concept at your job. While you will see direct benefits from reading this book, the greatest benefit you can carry away from it would be the exercise of learning to apply it.

Have fun!

Acknowledgments

We'd first like to thank Andy and Dave for letting us write a book for the Pragmatic Bookshelf. It has been a privilege to write a book for you. Andy, you especially went far and above the call of duty, spending hours with us tweaking the manuscript, giving us a crash course in writing, and occasionally (we're sure) grimacing over our. . . um. . . writing talent. Dave, you answered our many emails about the book rendering system and details of the markup language at all hours. Thanks to you both!

We had many great reviewers and contributors whose detailed and constructive feedback proved invaluable. We could not have produced this book without your time and expertise. Susan Henshaw and Jim Weiss took time to review some unpolished texts and read them more than once. Thank you.

Thanks also to Mike Clark, David Bock, Ken Pugh, Dominique Plante, Justin McCarthy, Al Chou, Bryan Ewbanks, Graham Brooks, Grant Bremer, Guerry Semones, Joe Fair, Mark Donoghue, Roberto Gianassi, Rob Sartin, Shae Erisson, Stefan Schmiedl, and Andy Lester. Some of you suffered through very early versions of the book, and after recently rereading what you read, we apologize. Seriously, all the feedback was great, and it helped us improve the book tremendously.

We've worked with many people throughout our career, but some had more of a direct impact on our work and therefore this book. We'd like to thank Jim Weiss, Randy Humes, Graham Wright, Flint O'Brien, Toby

Segaran, and John Wilbanks. Our current manager, Oita Coleman, encouraged and supported us as well. We are fortunate to work at a world-class company like SAS.

This book wouldn't have been possible without the wisdom and writings of agile development communities. We've read books and articles from the gurus of XP, Scrum, Crystal, and many other software philosophies. Without your hard work and dedication, the software industry would still be stuck in the dark ages of software development. We may not be out of the dark yet, but we're headed in the right direction. Your tireless work benefits us all.

The open-source community at large has given so many tools and ideas to the world that we must thank you as well. Most of the tools we discuss here are free to use because of the unselfish contributions made by developers all over the world. We'd like to single out the SourceForge team and the Apache Software Foundation. The services and tools you provide make us far more productive and have changed the world.

Finally and most importantly, we'd like to thank our Lord and savior Jesus Christ. To Him be the glory!

Jared Richardson and Will Gwaltney

From Jared

My wife, Debra, spent many hours and days working on this book. There were days and weeks when Debra spent more time in this book than Will or me. There were other days that she played the role of a single parent so I could work on the book. I honestly don't think this effort would have been completed without her help and support. Thank you!

My children, Hannah and Elisabeth, endured many nights and weekends with Daddy locked in his office, working on The Book. Thank you for your understanding and love!

From Will

Many, many thanks to my family, who put up with many long nights and weekends of writing and much griping when things were not going well. You all made the whole thing worthwhile.

We are what we repeatedly do.
Excellence, then, is not an act, but a
habit.
▶ Aristotle

Chapter 1

Introduction

Many software developers today are frustrated. They work long, hard hours, but their teams can't seem to finish the current project. It's not for lack of effort or desire; everyone on the team wants to wrap the project up cleanly, but no one knows how to pull it all together. It's very difficult to find the time to do the reading and experimentation to find out what works and how to make it work in your shop. Most people are too busy working to embark on this type of research.

That's where *Ship It!* steps in. This book is a collection of basic, practical advice that has been proven in the field, on multiple projects, and in companies of all sizes. It's what we've encountered that works. We're not consultants who were in and out in a few weeks; we worked day in and day out at these companies. We didn't get to drop in ideas that sounded good and then move off to the next engagement. When things didn't work, we were still there to see them fail. On the other hand, we also got to see when things went really well.

Some of these ideas have been blatantly lifted from well-known software methodologies, and we've tried to give credit where it's due. Other ideas were forged from blood, sweat, and tears. We've experimented with many tools, techniques, and best practices, and when something worked, we kept it. When it flopped, we tossed it. Very little you will see here is blindingly original (this is a Good Thing). Instead, we "stood on the shoulders of giants," selecting ideas from the best minds in the industry, and transformed them into what you see here.

Fifty to seventy percent of software teams today don't use basic, well-known software practices ([Cus03]). Quite often, this isn't because they don't know what to do but because they simply don't know how to get the practices started in the here and now. We'll show you how to sell management on each idea, lay out practical steps to get you started, and then offer warning signs to look for so you won't veer off-track.

Ship It! was written by developers who have been "in the trenches." This book is our experience, not theory, ranging from small startups to the largest privately held software company in the world. It's a methodology-agnostic, down-to-earth guide for making projects *work*.

We've tried to model the book after the popular Pragmatic Bookshelf titles: a practical, light, easy read. Our hope is to build on the foundation the other Pragmatic titles have begun.

1.1 Habitual Excellence

So how does Aristotle's quote fit here? "We are what we repeatedly do. Excellence, then, is not an act, but a habit." Excellence isn't defined by turning out one great product (or a number of great products). It comes out of what we do each day: our habits. *Extraordinary products are merely side effects of good habits.*

Applying this quote to ourselves (both professionally and personally) requires that we recognize our lives are side effects of our habits, so we'd better choose our habits carefully. Most people just randomly fall into their work routines, for a variety of reasons: this is how you learned it, it's how your boss used to do it, and so on. We can do better.

Purposely seek out good habits, and add them to your daily routine.

Try this experiment. Find a development methodology to research, and extract one habit that looks good to you (and that can be used by itself). Put it to use for a week. If you like it and it seems beneficial, continue using it for a month. Practice the new habit until it becomes a natural part of your routine, and then start the process all over again. Just as you lay a foundation brick by brick, repeat this process, and build a foundation of excellence one new habit at a time. Never be afraid to remove something that doesn't work in your circumstance, and don't keep a practice just because it's well-known or popular. Forge out your own way, based on what works for you and what doesn't.

"How we spend our days is, of course, how we spend our lives."[1] If that's so, then we must be careful how we spend our days.

---

[1]Annie Dillard (U.S. author, poet, and Pulitzer prize winner in 1975 for nonfiction)

```
╭─ Tip 1 ─╮
```

Choose your habits

Don't fall into habits by accident. Choose your habits deliberately.

1.2 A Pragmatic Point of View

This book is not an academic analysis of why something should or shouldn't work, and it isn't a catalog of available practices and methodologies that you can choose from.

Instead, this book presents what has worked for us on real-life software projects. We would introduce a new tool or practice and use it until it was evident whether it worked. We kept those that worked in our software development toolbox and carried them with us. Eventually, it actually appeared we knew what we were doing! We hope these tools and practices will work well for you also.

We've spent time in startups that didn't have the luxury of using a methodology simply because it was "the right one." Our circumstances forced us to find ideas that solved problems that we could put to work immediately. We've also worked in larger companies that had significant resources and technology at their disposal. We've found that even large companies don't want to use a tool just because it's elegant or because some guru endorses it. They want solutions that solve today's problems quickly and inexpensively. So we picked up a habit here, and dropped a habit there, until our toolkit was generic enough to be portable but still solved problems effectively. This book is a collection of good habits that we've used that will make a difference in your shop as well—the results can be astonishing.

To illustrate: let us tell you a Tale of Two Software Shops (with apologies to Charles Dickens).

The first shop was a mess. They'd purchased rather expensive source code management software but never installed it. As a result, they lost the source code for the demo they were showing to potential customers. No one was sure what features were supposed to be included in the product, but the entire development team was working on it nonetheless. The code was unstable and would crash every five minutes or so (usually at the worst possible moment—during live demos). This mess didn't do much for morale; company meetings regularly spiraled downward into shouting matches. Some developers avoided the situation by hiding in their offices all day long. All in all, it was a *bad* place to work. Everyone knew there were major problems, but nobody could fix them.

The second shop was in much better shape. With about the same number of developers, they were working on three major products simultaneously. These projects had their code in a source code management system; the code was automatically rebuilt and tested whenever it changed. The entire team had daily meetings that were short, professional, and effective. Every developer knew what features to work on because each project had a master plan. They followed the quarry worker's creed: *We who cut mere stones must always be envisioning cathedrals* [HT00]. That is, everyone was able to apply their own expertise and craft within the context of a larger, coordinated framework. Their products shipped on time with a minimum of fuss and bother and were stable because they were well-crafted.

The most amazing thing about these two companies is that they're the *same shop*, separated by less than six months and the application of the principles in this book. (But you had already guessed that, hadn't you?) After the turnaround, the CEO said we had introduced an "atmosphere of excellence" and that he "didn't even recognize the place." This company is one of the more recent places we've worked, and we brought the principles in this book to bear in almost the same form as we're presenting them to you. The transformation we went through there is one of the reasons we decided to write this book for you.

We've discovered and applied these ideas at companies of all sizes, from a four person startup to SAS, the largest privately owned software company in the world. Frankly, we've been amazed at how well these principles have worked at companies of all sizes.

Think of these ideas as the foundation to a great product. You'll reap benefits for the rest of the product's life cycle if you're willing to invest the time up front to get your infrastructure set up properly. Of course, it's easier to start a project with all of these practices in place. Like a cracked foundation of a house, some can be patched easily while others are deeply structural and can be a lot of work to go back and fix.

While you may be in the middle of a project currently, it's never too late to start good habits. You can introduce many of these ideas into an existing project and reap immediate benefits, and we'll cover ways to do that in the last chapter.

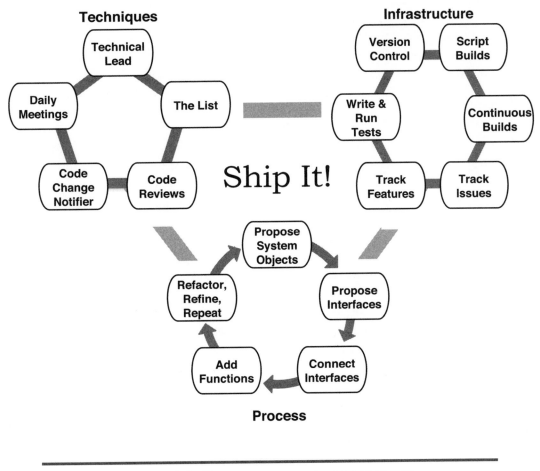

Figure 1.1: HOW TO BUILD A GREAT PRODUCT

1.3 Road Map

We have arranged our ideas into three main areas: infrastructure, techniques, and process (see Figure 1.1). These areas directly affect your team's ability to consistently deliver the product your customers want.

Infrastructure

In *Tools and Infrastructure* we cover the software tools that will make your life and your team's life easier. For instance, a good source code management system keeps the "crown jewels" of your project—your source code—safe and sound. An automated build system gives you repeatable builds anywhere and anytime you like. And we discuss how to keep track of the bug reports, feature requests, and other issues that come up the moment you let the rest of the world see what you've been developing. Finally, we show you how a good test harness can give you confidence that your code does what you think it does.

Techniques

In *Pragmatic Project Techniques* we cover specific practices that you and your team can use every day to "work smarter, not harder." We tell you how to put a tech lead on your team to insulate you from the outside world and to get you only the information you need to know. Use The List by yourself to organize your own work and teamwide to keep the group on-track. Is your team not communicating? Can't tell who's doing what? Start holding Daily Meetings to keep everyone on the same page while sneaking in some opportunities to pick teammates' minds. Short code reviews help leverage the expertise of your co-workers and let you share a little of your expertise too. And once the review is over, show the rest of your team what you've done with code change notifications.

Process

No book on software development would be complete without a presentation of the authors' pet development methodology, and this one is no different. So we humbly added a plug for what we call Tracer Bullet Development. When you use Tracer Bullet Development you create an end-to-end working system that's mostly stubbed out and then fill in the missing parts to make it real. It's good for splitting large projects apart and letting teams work on the pieces in parallel, and it also lends itself nicely to automated testing.

Common Problems and How to Fix Them

Finally, we present common problems—and danger signs—that arise and offer real-world advice on how to solve them using the tools, techniques, and processes we talk about in the rest of the book. A lot of these problems we encountered ourselves over the years. Some we solved, others we figured out how to solve after the fact (hindsight *is* 20/20, after all. . .). We hope our experience will keep you from making the same mistakes we made.

What's Missing?

People and requirements gathering are two areas that we didn't include. Good people trump tools, techniques, and process as the most important part of a project; however, assembling and keeping a great team is a subject worthy of its own book (or a series of books!). Instead, we focus on ways to leverage and grow the skills your team already has.

Similarly, learning about product requirements is another deep subject. There are many ways to collect requirements, ranging from note cards to complicated systems full of checks and balances. Rather than attempt to address another large issue that we couldn't do justice to in a single chapter, we chose to present ideas that are flexible enough to handle changing requirements, no matter where you get the requirements from. The ideas in this book can accommodate the project whose requirements never change as well as the project whose requirements are constantly shifting. So you can use these ideas whether you get your requirements list from a small stack of 3x5 cards or a 10,000-page contract.

We've tried to keep the discussions generic enough that you can use them in any shop and with any technology. That's why we didn't add sections on installer technologies or code optimizing tools.

1.4 Moving On

Our hope is that you will use the ideas and habits presented here in the spirit in which they were forged (i.e., pragmatically). Read them, and try them out. Keep what works in your environment, and discard the rest.

Stop after each section to determine whether you're using the idea. If you aren't, then read *How Do I Get Started?* If you are using the idea, read *Am I Doing This Right?* or *Warning Signs* to make sure you're on the right track.

1.5 How Should I Read This Book?

How you approach this book depends on your role in the project. Naturally, when you work as a developer or tester, you will approach the book differently than your team lead, but you can get a lot of value from this book when working in either role.

You Are a Developer or Tester

If you are a front-line practitioner (or implementor), read this book from front to back. Each section contains practical ideas you can use daily as an individual contributor or a team leader. Often developers skip sections with a team focus if they are not team leads. That's a really bad idea. Most team environments are a collection of what team members have requested or have had direct experience doing. Put yourself in a position to know what tools, techniques, and processes can make a positive impact in your shop and be able to present solid reasons for each request you make. Many times we've heard developers argue for a given tool or technique because "it's the right way." This argument never sways management and is, in fact, counterproductive. Before you present an idea, be sure to understand the benefit to the team.

Which request would sway you? "We need a source code management system from Acme Code Systems because it's a good thing and everyone is using it. It's a best practice!" or "We should have a source code management system because it will let us access past releases, roll back specific code changes and allow our developers to work on parallel code trees safely. It's the easiest way to safeguard our company's development investment. Acme Code Systems makes a great product that we should look at. Joe and I have been using it for several months now and it has made a real difference in our productivity. Here's a list of how it's helped us."

You Are a Project Team Lead

Use this book to perform an audit of your team's environment and work flow. (You do this from time to time already, right?) Take the opportunity to reexamine how your team works. Do you have a basic set of tools that cover your foundational requirements? Are your team's techniques building solid product and solid developers? Do you have a clean, well-defined process?

As you review how your team is working, be sure to consider each item's relevance. Are you using tools or practices that once fit but are no longer effective?

Did you hear the story of the woman who always cooked ham by cutting off and discarding a third of it first? When asked why, she said that was how her mother always cooked hams. When asked, her mother said that was how *her* mother had always cooked. They finally confronted

Grandma, who admitted that when she was young, she didn't have a pan big enough for an entire ham, so she always just cut the end off, and it became a habit.

Be sure that your habits are formed out of your needs today, not last year's project or Grandma's eccentricities.

Be sure that your team has access to the tools, techniques, and processes that it needs today. Knowing what works and why is the only way you can effectively guide your team. Each section has tips to help you get started and warning signs to alert you to problems before they get out of hand.

You Are a Manager (or Involved Customer)

Upper-level management can do a great deal to influence how teams work simply by asking for the right information. This book can show you some of the key components your teams should be using and what types of questions you should be asking. For example, when you ask for a list of fixes in the last release, you are saying that you want that information tracked. As you read each section, look for *deliverables* you *deliverables* can ask your team leads to submit that can guide them in the direction you want them to work. Be very careful with these requests, though; you don't want to create bureaucratic busywork for the teams. You want to guide with carefully placed requests.

Since you are removed from the day-to-day work, you will probably skim over the *How Do I Get Started?* sections, but you'll want to understand the what and why of each topic.

Individuals Make a Team

Nearly every concept in this book has been used by team members, entire teams, *and* managers. A team member is often the one who first uses the practice, proves its worth, and then shares it with the team. We have done this repeatedly ourselves and seen others do it, and you can do the same thing. Here's a story about someone who did just that.

The Rapid Growth of Agility Support Systems at CafePress.com
by Dominique Plante and Justin McCarthy

When we started working at CafePress.com early last year, management was enthusiastic about adopting agile practices, but the development environment lacked basic support systems required to make changes with confidence.

Enter the Create and Buy project—an extension of CafePress's core offering that allowed individuals to easily design and buy customized merchandise (t-shirts, mugs, etc.). This project was the first attempt at introducing an explicit business and persistence layer in addition to the web presentation layer. Most of the business and persistence tier was designed test first using the NUnit framework for writing developer tests. Simultaneously, we introduced NAnt for repeatable compilation and deployment of classes used in the web tier. Next, we wired up CruiseControl.NET for continuous integration (i.e., compile and run tests) upon every check-in to our Subversion code repository. For the finishing touch, we commissioned Chicken Little, a small but highly visible (and audible!) workstation running CCTray for build status notification.

The interoperability between Subversion, CruiseControl.NET, NAnt, and NUnit helped us evolve a hospitable collaboration environment without contentious vendor analysis or purchasing decisions. Moreover, these support systems were developer initiated, never because of explicit management requests.

Since we started doing all of this automation, our team has grown, and many new team members have advanced the maturity of our test suite and project automation tools. Some recent upgrades include 100 percent scripted development environment creation, as well as automated test environment deployment; although, looking back, `nant test` is still the most frequently used target.

Before the advent of these tools, most of our daily communication consisted of broadcasting questions about build failures or notifications of API changes. Now that CruiseControl.NET handles our "buddy builds," developers understand and honor a commitment to keeping the build pristine. Nobody enjoys a work stoppage because of an errant check-in. With the support systems in place, our conversations naturally trended toward software design and implementation and away from venting our environmental frustrations.

All of our early efforts aided the immediate delivery of tested code, and our initial investment continues to pay dividends every time Chicken Little squawks!

We feel this is the best way for change to occur. We would never discourage a manager from introducing change, but we find the best and most applicable changes come up from the trenches. The people doing the work usually have a good idea about what specific problems need to be solved.

So we say, "use the book" whether you are a manager, a developer, a tester, or a tech lead. Find the parts your shop (or your own personal work) is missing, and see how it can make your life a little easier today.

╲╎╱ Joe Asks...

What Is Agility?

Agility refers to a software team's ability to adapt to changing conditions quickly. This sometimes means redesigning to accommodate changing requirements, and other times it means responding to new bugs quickly or adopting new technologies quickly. Generally, agile teams are more concerned with results than bureaucracy. You can read more about agile software at http://www.agilemanifesto.org/.

The following quote from the web site sums up the agile point of view pretty well:

"We are uncovering better ways of developing software by doing it and helping others do it. Through this work we have come to value

- Individuals and interactions over processes and tools

- Working software over comprehensive documentation

- Customer collaboration over contract negotiation

- Responding to change over following a plan

That is, while there is value in the items on the right, we value the items on the left more."

. . . the cost of adding a feature isn't just the time it takes to code it. The cost also includes the addition of an obstacle to future expansion. . . . the trick is to pick the features that don't fight each other.

▶ John Carmack

Chapter 2

Tools and Infrastructure

There were once two men (Mike and Joe) who wanted to build a house. One man (Mike) first spent a lot of time and a decent amount of money buying tools and learning how to use them. The other man (Joe) took the tools he already had (a hammer and four screwdrivers) and started working. Not surprisingly, Joe's house got started faster. While Mike was learning how to use the air compressor and nail gun, Joe was hammering nails. However, once Mike got over his learning curve and started building, he passed Joe in no time. Mike was able to build a better house in a shorter amount of time by investing time and learning how to use his tools. And does anyone wonder who finished their next house faster?

Just like Mike, we have many tools at our disposal. We can be like Joe and make do with the tools that we already know, blinded by the need to work *right now!* or we can step back and evaluate how we work. Perhaps some of the tools in this chapter weren't available in the shops you've worked in, or maybe you worked in a shop that used the tools poorly, and that left a bad taste in your mouth. We encourage you to peruse this chapter and see if the tools we discuss can't make a positive impact on your daily routine.

Let's look at a day in the life of Fred, a typical developer in a typical shop. His work experience is affected a great deal by his environment—his shop's tools and infrastructure.

Nobody Knows The Trouble Fred Has Seen

When Fred arrives at work in the morning, he sees an email from Wilma about some code changes she made last evening. Since he needs those changes, Fred copies her code onto his machine from a network drive. After an hour of tinkering, he gets Wilma's work compiling on his machine. He spends a few minutes double-checking her changes, and they seem to be working. Then Fred looks at his notes from yesterday to refresh his memory. He was *almost* finished coding a new feature. After three days of working in this area, he figures he'll have it completed by lunch.

Eager to get to work, Fred fires up his code editor, but his changes are gone! A sinking feeling washes over him. Fred realizes that he copied Wilma's code on top of his own work. Three days of work was erased in thirty seconds, and there's no way to get it back. "Oh well," thinks Fred, "that's not the first time this has happened, and it won't be the last. . . it's just a hazard of the job."

Just then Richard from sales drops in to check on the progress of a bug fix that was requested last week. Fred winces. . . in the rush to add the new feature, he forgot to work on the bug. Richard isn't very happy about the delay, but Fred promises to finish it before the end of the day.

Fred finally gets the overdue bug fixed late in the afternoon. As he starts preparing an update to send the customer, he realizes the customer in question is using the previous version of the product, *not* the version that he just fixed. As the rest of the office starts packing up for the day, Fred calls his wife to cancel their dinner plans and then starts searching the network drives for a copy of the old code so he can move the fix to that version of the product.

After spending an hour or so locating the right version of the code, an hour getting it running on his machine, and then another hour moving the code fix to the old code base, Fred is done.

It has been a long day, but he's proud of the hours he puts in. Fred is willing to work as hard as he has to for the company to succeed! His family is not always so understanding, though.

The next day the customer discovers that Fred accidentally reintroduced an old bug to the product, and introduced two new ones.

How Is Your Day Different?

Let's drop you into Fred's situation. You arrive in the morning and find email from Betty telling you about her code changes. Your shop uses a source code management (SCM) package that stores all code changes in a central repository, and downloads changes as needed. So you just ask your SCM for Betty's updates, and they're merged into the code already on your machine. If there are any collisions or code overwrites, the SCM warns you before any changes are lost.

Next, you issue a one-line build command, and Betty's changes compile right alongside your code. Since your shop uses a standard build system, Betty builds the code in the same way you do. Unlike Fred, you don't have to spend an hour getting the code to compile on your machine.

As you start working, Richard from sales drops in to ask about the bug fix from last week. Like Fred, you had forgotten to work on it, but you're in the habit of checking the weekly report from your team's bug tracking software, and it had reminded you about it on Monday. You've fixed the bug, and the update is ready for the customer. Richard is pleased and goes away thinking good thoughts about you.

When you fixed the bug, you had to find the corresponding source code because this customer wasn't using the current version. You asked the SCM software to give you the older version, and it did. No time was spent searching network drives for code, and no bugs were accidentally reintroduced by old code trees.

Even if you had used a buggy tree, part of your build process includes running an automated test suite. This suite runs a lightweight set of tests designed to catch common bugs. If bugs are reintroduced, you'll catch them before the customer ever sees them.

At the end of the day, you leave work on time and take your family out for a nice dinner. Fred is working late, and his wife is annoyed once again. You finished the three-day feature addition and can move on to another task when you come back to work the next day. You're more productive than Fred, but you aren't smarter or more committed—you're both very dedicated, intelligent developers.

The only difference between you and Fred is that your shop put a few key tools to work and Fred's shop did not. Put these tools in place, and you'll have a solid development infrastructure that turns many common headaches into nonissues.

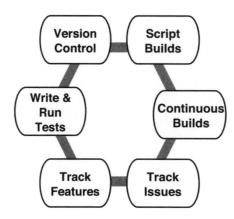

Figure 2.1: TOOLS AND INFRASTRUCTURE

Avoid the Fred Trap

Fred is so busy fixing bugs and fighting fires that he doesn't realize there's a better way. Every successful project has a strong basic framework in place: its infrastructure. These are the tools and practices your team uses to craft products, such as source code management systems and build tools. The specific tools you use may differ, but the categories are common for any project. This chapter describes the foundational tools that you should use on every project.

Some topics in this chapter may seem blatantly obvious, but we've included them despite that. Just because a topic is obvious doesn't mean it's widely used—or that it's used correctly.

Some teams may be well-equipped in most areas but will have huge blind spots in others. They can miss major tool categories entirely, despite spending enormous amounts of money on other areas—relying on vendors' claims of "supertools" that will do everything for them.

Bearing that in mind, as you finish each section, stop and compare what you just read with what you currently do. If you're not using the tool or idea, ask yourself, why not? Is it something you've never heard of, is it something you have little experience with, or does it just not work for you? If you are using the tool or idea, are you using it in the right spirit? If not, what would it take to do it better?

Develop in a Sandbox

How do you share code with your teammates? A surprising number of teams never answer this question explicitly and instead just get a big, old shared disk drive, with all of their source code and other files lying around. Any act by any developer—from simply editing a file to compiling code—will instantly affect every other developer on the team. Their life is now filled with constant, unpleasant surprises.

It's just like a crowded kitchen on Thanksgiving, with everyone throwing something else into the mix, and it makes for a pretty frustrating work environment. While many teams continue to operate this way, you can take a safer and more professional stand. This will have a deep effect on your tools and infrastructure, so you need to get this straight right from the beginning.

There's only one fundamental rule to keep in mind: isolate others from the effect of your work until you are ready. That's why we call this *sandbox development*: every developer has their own sandbox to play in without disturbing other developers.

That may sound easy enough, especially in terms of isolating source code (see Practice 2, *Manage Assets*, on page 20), but the real trick is to remember that it applies to *all* resources: source code, database instances, web services on which you depend, and so on.

Your own development machine should be designed to contribute to your own productivity.[1] It should not contribute anything to the global build process—no one else should have to rely on your machine directly for anything.

But how do other developers get your code? Code is shared via the *repository*. Think of the repository as a big shared disk, but one that's managed by a librarian. The librarian ensures that everyone has the right version of any file (or other resource) that they need and that everyone can work without clobbering each other. Every developer uses a software tool to check in and check out files (just like a real book library) so they can work on them locally. *repository*

On your own developer machine, you edit local copies of source code files, compile, build, and test in splendid isolation from your team-

---

[1] This means it's perfectly okay for different developers to use different code editors or even Integrated Development Environments (IDEs).

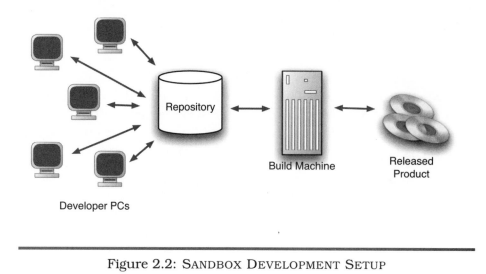

Figure 2.2: Sandbox Development Setup

mates. If you need to use a database, a web server, or any other resource while developing, make sure that you're the *only* one using it. When you're satisfied that you're finished with a piece of code, you check it back into the repository.

build machine

release

But then how do customers get the finished product? In addition to the developer machines and the repository, you have a *build machine*. The build machine is an unattended server that simply gets all of the latest source code from the repository, builds, and tests it, over and over again. The result of this build is the product *release*.

Most of the time, this release will just be thrown away after each build, but every so often this is the pile of bits that you'll ship to your customers and end users. It's built the same whether it's the usual 10:00 a.m. build or it's the final release after months of toil and sweat.

It's always consistent, because the build machine is an independent entity: it never looks at individual developer machines for any reason. The input to the build is the repository, and the output from the entire process is from a designated build machine. This system works great as long as developers don't cheat.

Tip 2

Stay in the sandbox

> ### $\overset{\text{\footnotesize \}/\}}{\underset{\sim}{\curvearrowright}}$ Joe Asks...
>
> #### Where Do Releases Come From?
>
> Your build machine may or may not be the box where you build releases—the code that you ship to your customers. However, the build box and the shipping product build box both use the same scripts, use the same repository as their source, and so on.
>
> Some of the differences might be that a shipping build creates a new branch or tag within the repository to mark a known, released set of code, or perhaps that the shipping build wraps the code in installers for various platforms.

Sometimes it's hard to "stay in the sandbox," especially if database licenses or web server ports are in short supply. You may be able to use a single database but create separate instances for each developer. Or, if forced to use one database with one instance, you may be able to partition the data space (for example, Joe is assigned test account data for accounts 1000–1999, and Sue is assigned accounts 2000–2999, and so on). This still leaves you open to risk of interference, but it's better than nothing.

For other resources such as web services, every developer should have a clear shot at their own instance (whether they are providing the service or testing against it).

With this basic idea of isolation in mind, let's take a look at some of the tools and other bits of infrastructure you'll need to achieve the sandbox effect.

Manage Assets

asset management

Most corporations have large systems and staff dedicated to *asset management*. That is, they keep track of all of the corporation's valuable physical assets—computers, cars, buildings, office staplers, and so on. On a software project, you have a somewhat simpler task: all you need to keep track of are files. But you need to keep track of every version of every file used in the build, from the beginning of the project onward.

For this formidable task, you need a *source code management* (SCM) system, also called a *version control* (VC) system. These systems act as gifted librarians, keeping track of all of your assets (files) in a repository (or database) and coordinating safe access to your files. These systems store your source code, of course, but also archive all the other supporting files, such as graphics, build scripts, XML droppings, documentation, and that little (but important) Perl script that everyone relies on.

With a properly set up SCM system, you can

- "Give your team a projectwide undo button; nothing is final, and mistakes are easily rolled back" [TH03].

- Handle conflicts when more than one person edits (or wants to edit) a given file at the same time.

- Track multiple versions of your software; you can add features to the next release while someone else fixes bugs in a previous release.

- Record which files are changed (when and by whom).

- Take a historical peek: you can retrieve a snapshot of your work from any given day.

If your entire development shop goes up in flames, you should be able to recover with just a backup of your repository. You should have everything you need to build the entire product; if you don't, then perhaps you aren't using the tool properly.

TIP 3
If you need it, check it in

Some people exempt third-party items, like the Java runtimes (which Sun makes freely available) or other specific products. They don't store these items in their SCM system. That may be fine if your product can run with various versions of a third-party product. However, if you depend on a specific version of that product, be aware that you are playing the odds that some other company will continue to provide and support that product version for you.

The only exception to the "Keep everything you need to build your product in the SCM" tip are files you can generate. If you have a set of 150 libraries (stored as JAR or DLL files) that are built from other products internal to your company, it would be silly to store those libraries in your SCM. You can rebuild them if needed because you have the original code in your SCM. However, if your 150 libraries are all from other companies, and you can't build your product without them, include them in your SCM.

Another point to consider is that products (and entire companies, for that matter) often disappear. If your vendor goes out of business or the supporters of your open-source tool decide to stop supporting the product, can you survive? Can your product still ship if a key vendor goes out of business or if an open-source project goes away? Products, both open-source and commercial, often disappear unexpectedly.

Be sure you have everything you need to build, deploy, and run your product in your source code management system. If you don't, you are putting the long-term viability of your development project at risk in order to save disk space.

Sounds kind of silly when you phrase it that way, doesn't it?

When you use an SCM, you can get to a specific version of your product (or to the current version, for that matter). You can roll back specific changes. When you work this way, your development hours aren't accidentally lost. Your work is too valuable to be overwritten and wiped out; store it in a source code system that lets you roll back changes and return to known good versions of your code.

The Dog Ate my Source Code

Do you know where your product's source code is? *All of it?* For every version? Are you sure? And are you sure that the rest of your team knows as well?

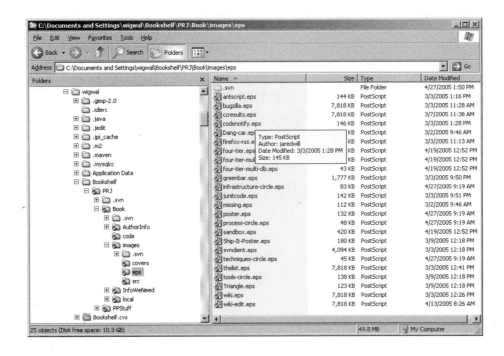

Figure 2.3: REVISION CHANGES SHOWN IN A SUBVERSION GUI CLIENT

Case in point: a small dot-com startup we joined had spent six figures on a state-of-the-art source code control system (ah, the joys of venture capital!). But they hadn't gotten around to installing it yet. Each of the three (yes, only three) developers had significantly different versions of the product code, with their own unique sets of bugs.

None of those versions matched the demo the company showed to prospective customers. After a major effort to reconcile the different versions, we eventually just gave up and picked one version to use going forward.

We installed the SCM, put this version of the code into it, and used it diligently from then on. Everybody *knew* which code was the "real" product code, and the developers' peace of mind (and the product's quality) improved dramatically.

How Do I Get Started?

If you're not using any type of source code control for your project, make it your top priority.

According to a recent survey, some 40 percent of IT shops in the United States do not use any source code or version control product at all, so we know you're out there [Zei01].

1. Evaluate a few SCM systems (see Appendix B on page 165). We heartily recommend CVS or Subversion (see Figure 2.3 on the preceding page for an example).

   Both are free and used by some of the largest software companies in the world. If you choose a commercial solution, these products will still give you a baseline to compare their feature sets against.

2. Learn how to use your SCM.

3. Generate a single-page quick-start guide that shows how to use the system for common operations. (Check the lists on page 35 for warning signs, etc.)

4. Show the system to your team. Be sure everyone is comfortable with the system.

5. Import your code and supporting files.

6. Start keeping all your files in the SCM.

Am I Doing This Right?

First, are you actively using the system? If you go weeks—even days—between code check-ins, you aren't using the system actively. This defeats the whole purpose (backing up your work and maintaining an accurate fine-grained history). Even if your code isn't ready for the production tree, it can be placed in a private or personal area of the system.

If the hard drive on your workstation crashed right now, how much work would you lose? If it's more than a day or two, consider changing the way you work.

Also, how long would it take you to get a new machine up and running for development? Are all of your build scripts and development resources checked in?

Can you perform SCM operations quickly? If it takes you twenty minutes to check out code and another fifteen minutes to put changes back in, you won't do check-ins frequently. Your basic interactions must be fast.

Operations such as fetching differences can put a heavy load on the CPU and disk drives. Quite often companies will put their SCM software on an antiquated computer, making all interactions painful.

Hardware is cheap, but developer time is expensive. Whatever it takes (training, hardware, or new SCM software), be sure that your SCM is fast enough to keep up with you.

Are you backing up the SCM's repository? If the building burns down tonight, do you have an off-site backup that you can use to restore to another machine? A great SCM does you no good if the data it's storing gets lost. Be sure you are getting a complete, weekly off-site backup at a minimum.

Finally, do you know your system well enough to perform these basic operations easily? Here's a minimal list of operations that you need to know:

- Check out the entire project.

- Look at the differences between your edits and the latest code in the SCM.

- View the history for a specific file—who changed this file and when did they do it?

- Update your local copy with other developers' changes.

- Push (or commit) your changes to the SCM.

- Remove (or back out) the last changes you pushed into the SCM.

- Retrieve a copy of the code tree as it existed last Tuesday.

Warning Signs

- No activity in the repository. An unused repository is a useless repository. You should see activity every hour through the day as individual developers check in and check out regularly.

- Incomplete repository. If the repository contains only some of the files needed to build your product, it's not pulling its weight.

Beware of "experimental" release or test trees that aren't being stored in the repository or of contents of critical XML files or databases.

- Slow access. If it takes a long time to check in or check out files, people will eventually stop using it—even if they are using it now.

- Lost files, corrupted files. Some version control systems (made by certain large, unnamed companies) are known to "eat" files on a regular basis. Upgrade to a real system, such as the freely available CVS[2] or Subversion.[3]

---

[2]http://www.cvshome.org
[3]http://subversion.tigris.org

Script Your Build

build

A *build* converts source code into a runnable program. Depending on the computer language and environment, this may mean you're compiling source code and/or bundling images and other resources together as needed. The scripts, programs, and technologies used by your compile and resource bundling are all combined to create the build system.

Now remember we're not talking about compiling/building within your IDE. For the most part, you do *not* want to use your personal developer IDE to compile the project, even if you're the only one using it (see Practice 1, *Develop in a Sandbox*, on page 17 if this sounds odd to you). We're talking about a build on your own machine that parallels the "official" build on the build machine. Here's a little story to explain why.

Billy is ready to build his product, so he fires up his IDE and opens what he believes to be the right project. He asks the IDE to rebuild his project. When the IDE is done, he exits and copies the program to his installer directory. He then opens up his install program, points it at the program, and tells it to build an installer.

Once the installer is built, he runs it to make sure it works. The installer immediately crashes. Billy remembers that he has forgotten to copy the latest version of the third-party `Widgets` that his product depends on. So he copies the latest version of `Widgets` into his installer directory. After he has built the program a second time, he realizes he forgot to copy over the latest version of the graphics his program uses. . . .

Feels like a marathon, doesn't it? Billy is having a long night and yet again putting in some more unpaid overtime and missing reruns of *Buffy*.

Bob is also building his product today. Bob goes to the folder containing his code and types a one-line command (for instance, ant build_installer or make all) to run his build script. The script builds the product (automatically fetching everything the product depends on), builds an installer for it, and tests the installer. Bob is now done.

You can see from these scenarios the difference between using an automated build system and assembling your product by hand. Billy made a lot of errors that Bob avoided by automating his build. The steps that

Billy forgot to perform were done automatically for Bob by his script, which does things the same way every time.

While many people will see Billy working late and consider him to be the more dedicated employee, we would rather work with (or be!) Bob. Automating your process not only makes your steps more exact (and less likely to be error-prone) but also lets you leave work on time—like Bob.

You can build your product in a variety of ways. You could have a list of steps that looks something like this:

1. Compile your code.

2. Copy the compiled code to your installer program.

3. Move the latest copy of your third party libraries (e.g., database drivers and parsers).

4. Drop in your non-code files such as HTML and graphics.

5. Copy over your help files to the installer.

6. Build the installer.

You have a problem if you do *anything* by hand in your build or packaging process. The only question is whether you choose to invest the time to address the problem up front or you waste time performing the task by hand over and over and then deal with the problems that result from the inevitable mistake when a step is missed or blundered. The first option is a wise investment of your time in the early stages of a project. The second is a black hole. It will be a source of frustration and problems for the life of your product. In other words, you'll have to work much harder to build a solid house if you skimp on the foundation.

TIP 4

Script builds on day one

At a minimum, use a batch file or shell script to perform the build (there are better ways to do this, of course, and you'll start looking at those shortly).

But wait! you cry, why can't I just use my IDE to perform these steps for me? Well, you could, but here are the issues:

- It's unlikely that the build machine is using the same IDE (most IDEs make it cumbersome, or even impossible, to operate in a batch mode).

- You would have to force your entire team—experts and beginners alike—to use the same IDE. Sometimes that's acceptable, but many times it raises more problems than it solves.

- Even when everyone uses the same IDE, it can be difficult to propagate changes in the development environment (a new library, a different compiler setting) to everyone.

These problems aren't insurmountable, but they are sticky. That's why we find it much easier to separate the automation of the build from the IDE world. But it's important that the build—in all its complexity—can be launched with a single command.

If you can't build your project with a single command, then most of the team won't bother. As is true of most tasks, nobody will do it if it isn't easy. One of the hallmarks of a great development effort is being able to build your project easily (and consistently) on every developer's desktop.

Much as we'd like, it doesn't always go that way. In one shop from our checkered past, they always built their product by hitting the Build button inside a specific IDE on a certain machine. Then the developer who had set up the build left the company. None of the remaining employees knew how to build the system without using the departed developer's workstation and its "magic Build button." The managers were shocked when we told them how the code was built—they had no idea.

Be sure you can build your product the same way on every workstation in the shop. If you don't know how to build the product, the odds are good that no one else does either.

> TIP 5
> **Any machine can be a build machine**

In a pinch, any developer's box can substitute for the build box by using the same (checked-in) scripts. The goal is that a build on any capable machine should be bit-for-bit identical with that of the build machine (except for things like time stamps, the IP address or name of the machine, etc.)

Build scripts don't have to be very complicated. This example shows a complete and usable Ant script that's still pretty straight-forward and readable (despite the XML angle brackets).

```xml
<?xml version="1.0" ?>
<project name="SimpleExample" default="doall">
        <property name="build.dir" value="./build" />
        <property name="dist.dir" value="./dist" />

        <target name="init">
                <mkdir dir="${build.dir}" />
                <mkdir dir="${dist.dir}" />
        </target>

        <target name="compile" depends="init">
                <javac srcdir="."
                            destdir="${build.dir}"/>
        </target>

        <target name="dist" depends="compile">
                <jar destfile="${dist.dir}/SimpleExample.jar"
                        compress="true">
                            <fileset dir="${build.dir}" />
                </jar>
        </target>

        <target name="doall" depends="dist">
        </target>
</project>
```

How Do I Get Started?

If you just inherited a new product without an automated build, you should take these steps immediately to get a build script in place:

1. Have a team member manually build the system while you take notes.

2. Define the individual build steps.

3. Pick a build tool but be prepared to revisit other options if this tool becomes too burdensome.

4. Incrementally script each step; eliminate manual operations one by one.

5. Run the script on another workstation. This step will catch any accidental workstation-specific code.

6. Now have another team member try to use the script without your help.

When you complete these steps, you will have a script that should work for everyone.

Am I Doing This Right?

If you're using your manual build system properly, you will be able to build your entire product:

- With one command

- From your Source Code Management system (SCM)

- On any team member's workstation

- With no external environmental requirements (such as specific network drives)

If you have issues with any of these items, have another look at your build process.

Warning Signs

- Your build contains *any* manual steps.

- Your build script has to be modified to run on different machines.

- Only a few team members know how to edit the build script.

Build Automatically

An unattended build is an automatic one. However, before you can implement an automatic build, you must already have a manual build system in place that you can run with a single command. If you don't have that, back up to Practice 3, *Script Your Build*, on page 26. You can't automate a process that doesn't exist.

Once you can build your product automatically, how often should you do so? Ideally, you will rebuild every time the code changes. That way you'll know immediately if any change broke your build. Add a light-weight set of *smoke tests* to this system, and you also get a basic level of functional insurance as well. This type of system is called *Continuous Integration*.[4] A Continuous Integration (or CI) tool sits on a clean, nondeveloper box (the build machine) and rebuilds your project every time someone commits code. Rebuilding each time code is committed keeps your code base clean by catching compile errors as soon as they occur. It also runs your test suites to catch functional errors. We use an open-source CI tool called CruiseControl[5] because it's well-supported, it scales well, and it's free!

smoke tests

Continuous Integration

Unfortunately, most development shops (nearly 70 percent [Cus03]) don't even bother with a daily build, let alone a CI system. Those shops that do have a CI system are among the best, consistently turning out better code and more stable products. You might argue that the shops most likely to introduce this type of technology are fairly advanced and therefore turn out better code. We disagree!

We believe that the benefit comes from having a constant "virtual build monitor" that catches every bad code commit almost immediately. It always flags code that doesn't compile. It also catches the new files that you forgot to add or the existing files you modified. Automated build systems are great at catching the details that we humans are so good at missing.

> **TIP 6**
>
> Build continuously

---

[4] http://martinfowler.com/articles/continuousIntegration.html
[5] CruiseControl is an open-source Continuous Integration system hosted at Source-Forge.net. http://cruisecontrol.sourceforge.net/

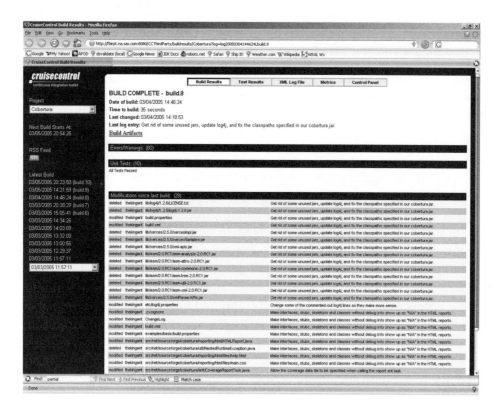

Figure 2.4: CRUISECONTROL STATUS REPORT WEB PAGE

bug regression

You can also move beyond "Does it compile?" and ask "Does it run?" With a well-selected test suite, basic functionality is retested and bugs are not allowed to be reintroduced (preventing *bug regression*). With this system, your development staff spends their time adding features instead of fixing compile failures or refixing the same bugs again and again. It is impossible for manual testing to give developers this level of coverage. The immediate feedback on every code change catches problems quickly so that issues can be fixed quickly. This is one of the biggest reasons that shops with CI systems are consistently superior to others.

Put your shop in this category! It's easier than you think, and the benefits are enormous.

\\// **Joe Asks...**

What Is Bug Regression?

Bug Regression is when an issue that you've fixed sneaks back in your code. This problem happens when you accidentally put bad code back into the SCM (after the problem has been fixed), or when the same mistake is reintroduced. Regression bugs are quite a frustrating issue.

If you write a test for every bug you fix and run it in your CI system, the system catches Bug Regressions when the offending code is checked in. This strategy effectively stops Bug Regressions.

TIP 7

Test continuously

At SAS, the largest privately owned software company in the world (and coincidentally our employer), there are more than five million lines of code under a CI system. In fact, there are generally multiple branches getting this coverage, so it's really a multiple of five million lines of code being monitored! (See our story in [Cla04].) If CI works on that scale, it can work in your shop too.

Are CI systems really worth it? Well, at one rather large company in our experience there was one key project whose build failure caused cascading problems that caused nearly 150 other projects across the company to fail the overnight builds. A CI system caught the error early in the afternoon, but the system was in beta and not being monitored, so nearly 150 projects did not build that night. This little glitch impacted development teams on several continents. Shortly after this incident, management accelerated the companywide roll out of the CI system to prevent these kinds of errors.

Presentation

Once you decide to set up a CI system, give some thought to how you want to present the results. Every CI system lets you publish your results to HTML (see Figure 2.4 on the preceding page). Most also let you send email (Practice 14, *Send Code Change Notifications*, on page 98) as well. However, this is just the tip of the iceberg. With a little extra tweaking, your systems can display their results in more interesting ways.

Enable RSS feeds (see the sidebar on page 62) for your build system. This pushes out the build information to subscribers without making them wade through constant email.

Add lava lamps! Most build systems can use X10 modules[6] to drive any visual device you have. Some people use lava lamps,[7] and others prefer an Ambient Orb,[8] but you can drive whatever you like. Try to have fun with your notifications.

How Do I Get Started?

You must already have a good build system in place to move to the next level with an automated build system.

1. Select an automatic build system to use. Do *not* write your own.[9]

2. Obtain a "clean" machine to run on.

3. Install your automatic build system, and configure it for your environment. *Document every step of the install.*

ROI

That's it! You can set up this type of system fairly easily, and the return on investment (known to management as *ROI*) usually reaches the break-even point in the first few months. If management doesn't see the benefit, run the system on your own machine at first. People who have never used a CI system often need a live demonstration to appreciate how powerful the concept is.[10]

---

[6]X10 modules allow you to control electrical switches from your computer. People use them to drive all sorts of devices, from lights to lava lamps. Check them out at http://x10.com.

[7]Like Mike Clark. http://www.pragmaticprogrammer.com/pa/pa.html

[8]Michael Swanson's blog is at http://blogs.msdn.com/mswanson/articles/169058.aspx.

[9]We've seen many people try to bolt together a quick notification system, but why do that when you can use a fully tested enterprise-level CI system for free? You won't add half the features or reports that a full-blown project will have. See Appendix D on page 173 for a listing of CI products. After all, reinventing the wheel is not pragmatic.

[10]For a quick head start, check out Mike Clark's movie of CruiseControl in action at http://media.pragprog.com/movies/auto/CruiseControl_MikeClark.html.

> ### If a Tree Falls in the Woods...
>
> The best automatic build system in the world is useless if you don't look at the results. Most systems automatically send email; take advantage of this feature! We have seen a great deal of resistance to this feature up front, but we've also seen the most acceptance (and benefit) from the emails once the teams acclimate to them. You'll come to depend on these notices and will eventually not leave for the day until the *All Is Well* message arrives.

Am I Using This Right?

If you're using an automatic build system (or a CI system), you are far ahead of most software teams. But there are still a few questions you need to ask yourself:

- Do you have tests in the system? After all, no one cares if it compiles if it doesn't run.

- Is anyone paying attention to the system? Are the notifications turned on?

- Does your build get fixed quickly or stay broken for days?

- Does your build finish in a reasonable time, or does it take too long to complete?

If you can answer these questions favorably, your team will be able to spend their days adding features instead of tracking down which line of code broke feature X sometime during the last six months!

Warning Signs

- Your automatic build system breaks frequently.

- Your team ignores broken builds.

- The build stops running, and no one notices.

Track Issues

An issue list is a pretty simple concept: when someone reports a bug or other important issue, you want to keep a copy of that report around so you don't forget it. Pretty straightforward, right? (And since developers often get squeamish when we talk about *bugs*, we'll use the blander and more politically correct term *issue*.)

However, there can be more to keeping track of an issue than just the description of the issue itself. Keeping track of and effectively communicating details about issues can be tricky. You need to know the following:

- What version of the product has the issue?

- Which customer encountered the issue?

- How severe is it?

- Was the problem reproduced in-house (and by whom, so they can help you if you're unable to reproduce the problem)?

- What was the customer's environment (operating system, database, etc.)?

- In what version of your product did the issue first occur?

- In what version of your product was it fixed?

- Who fixed it?

- Who verified the fix?

Over time, you'll notice you are outgrowing the white board or 3x5 cards; a project's complexity increases very quickly. While these mediums can certainly hold the information, they cannot search on it or publish it on a web page for your tech support team. They do not scale well or share well. Instead, keep this information in a database.

With the database, tech support can quickly look up an issue when a customer calls in. They'll be prepared to tell customers you're already aware of the issues and whether the problems are fixed in the next version (see Figure 2.5 on the next page for an example).

You'll create a long-term, productwide (and even companywide) memory. The alternative is a kind of corporate Alzheimer's disease: issues

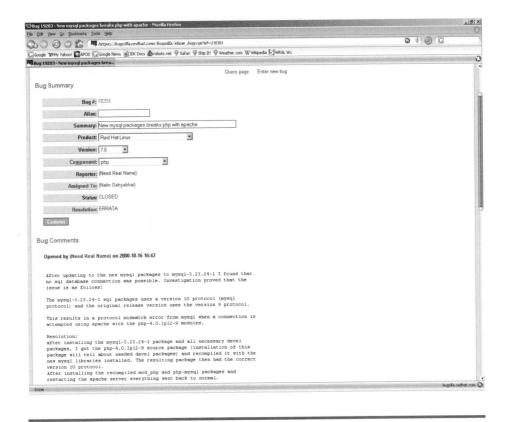

Figure 2.5: EXAMPLE ISSUE TRACKER INPUT SCREEN

that are discovered will continue to be rediscovered the hard way, wasting time and frustrating your customers as well as your testing staff and developers.[11]

> TIP 8
>
> Avoid collective memory loss

A good issue tracking system will generate activity reports for a given product. How many issues were entered? How many issues were fixed, and how long did it take, etc.? These sorts of reports can be used to identify trouble spots in the project. (Studies show that bugs,

---

[11]It has been said that customers will forgive nearly any problem, as long as you tell them about it in a known-issues list. If your customers have to tell you about your own bugs, they forgive nothing.

ahem, *issues*, tend to clump near each other—rarely are they evenly distributed.)

You can also use your tracking system to generate to-do lists for development staff, as well as known-issues lists for the product. If no one is fixing issues, it's pointless to waste time finding them.

Consider the case of Harry and Lloyd, intrepid developers, working at a small software startup. When we met them, they tracked every issue via Post-it Notes stuck on the wall above their desks. These little pieces of paper were their *only* way of tracking bugs, and they assured us this system worked fine. We still insisted that we use a standard issue tracking package. We got some resistance and comments about fixing what isn't broken, but they humored us and we transitioned into the new system.

Now this company had a very large customer, one of the reference accounts, who called in one day and wanted to know when issue X would be fixed. They said they had reported this issue two releases back and were tired of waiting patiently. They wanted to know why we were ignoring them. Harry and Lloyd insisted that they had never heard of the issue and that the customer was simply confused. We eventually fixed the issue, and the customer became less angry, but we never got that account back to the level of "raving fan."

Six months later, while moving Harry's desk, we found a Post-it Note on the floor, right where it had fallen. Written in big, red letters was *IMPORTANT! DO NOT FORGET!* followed by the customer's issue. Once it fell behind the desk, the "out of sight, out of mind" rule kicked in, and they forgot the issue. When you use an issue tracking system, you provide yourself with a safety net that Harry and Lloyd never had.

Your issue tracking system is a bookkeeping detail. You need it to track what you've worked on, what you have and haven't fixed, and what you plan to fix. A white board, index cards, or a spiral-bound notebook might handle your needs for a few months but not for any length of time, and these certainly don't scale to the enterprise.

How Do I Get Started?

If you don't currently have an issue tracking system, don't wait. Don't delay your transition until you can transfer every issue ever encountered. That's an admirable goal, but don't wait until you have your manual system clean before using the automated system. Just start using it as soon as you can. Enter the new issues in your new system, and over time it will achieve the critical mass of information that makes it a vital resource. If you have the time to populate the new system, great! But don't make it a requirement for use.

1. Pick an issue tracking system (Appendix E, on page 177).
2. Set up a test system for yourself, and learn how to use it.
3. Generate a one-page quick-start guide for your internal users.
4. Start keeping all new issues in this system.
5. Move pre-existing issues over to the new system as time permits.

Am I Doing This Right?

If you track issues with any sort of a system, you're doing great. The real question is whether you store enough information in the system and whether anyone uses the system internally. Use these questions to gauge your success:

- Can you generate a list of the top-priority, unaddressed issues? How about the second-tier issues?

- Can you generate a list of last week's fixes?

- Can your system reference the code that fixed the issue?

- Do your tech leads use this system to generate to-do lists for development teams?

- Does your technical support team know how to get information out of the system?

- Can your system notify "interested parties" so tech support (and others) can see when an issue is fixed?

Warning Signs

- The system isn't being used.

- Too many small issues are in the system.

- Issue-related metrics are used to evaluate team member performance.[12]

---

[12]This is a slippery slope. It's tempting to say that someone who reports or fixes more issues is more productive, but using metrics to evaluate performance won't work. If you award raises based on the number of issues entered, your system will quickly be filled with irrelevant, nit-picking bugs.

> ### It's Not a Bug, It's a Feature!
>
> The short definition of a *bug* (a.k.a. *an issue*) is something in your software that doesn't do what you meant for it to do. This definition covers problems from data loss and system crashes to simple spelling errors.
>
> A feature, on the other hand, is an improvement to an existing product. Never let an overzealous sales or marketing group classify improvements as bugs, attempting to raise their favorite features to a higher priority. The feature can be assigned an appropriate priority if it is important. Reclassifying it as a bug simply pollutes the system.

Track Features

feature

A new *feature* in your product refers to added functionality. It's making your product do something that it didn't do before. For example, making your product talk to a different vendor's database is a feature. On the other hand, making your product work properly with a supported database is fixing a bug. The two are different and need to be treated differently.

There are many reasons you should track your feature requests accurately. You can gauge customer demand for new features, as well as generate to-do lists for the next product versions. Knowing who requested a feature is also crucial to prioritization. You can properly prioritize your feature list if you know that your smallest customer requested one feature but six of your largest customers requested another. You may add both features, but it's important to have a way of ordering the work.

You will likely forget about some features if you don't track them, and that will make the client who requested them believe you just don't care. That's not a good message to send.

Track features the same way you track your issues list. Keep a unified list of your feature requests. Prioritize them, and keep a basic estimate of the time involved to investigate or add the feature. You may also want to keep a list of the top items on your white board for better visibility.

Beware of Feature Creep

Many products hit the 90 percent done mark and never get finished. They always have just a few more features to finish or complete. Somehow, no matter how much the development teams get done, the product is never quite ready to ship. These products are suffering from a malady known as *feature creep*. Simply put, features keep getting added. Existing features keep being improved but never completed. Eventually you have to realize that you are "sanding through the finish."* You need a way to decide when to stop polishing and actually ship the product. To address this problem, be absolutely sure every feature and bug has a solid priority attached to it. Attaching a priority to everything you work on makes it easier for management to draw a line on the prioritized list and decide what ships and what doesn't. It's no longer an arbitrary decision or personal preference; it's based on the importance of the changes to the tech leads, the sales group, and, ultimately, the customers.

In the same vein, you should never work on anything that isn't on a list with an assigned priority (see Practice 10, *Work from The List*, on page 57).

---

*"Sanding through the finish" is a woodworking term. It refers to sanding a piece of furniture to add a polished look. However, there is a very real danger of sanding so much that you go right through the finish and start to damage the wood: a mistake common among novices.

Issue and feature lists are often kept in the same tracking system. Just be sure you have a clear and defined way to separate the lists. If you can't generate separate lists of outstanding feature requests and outstanding bugs for your product, you have a problem. If you must, use two separate products, but it is not required. Most tools can make this distinction.

There's an old saying, "If you don't write it down, it never happened." Even better than writing it down, have the computer keep track of it for you. If you don't, it may be as if it never happened. . . .

How Do I Get Started?

Getting started here is pretty much the same as *How Do I Get Started?* in the *Issue Tracking* section (see Practice 5, *Track Issues*, on page 36).

Am I Doing This Right?

You're in good shape if the following is true:

- You use this system as a first stop when it's time to generate the next release's feature list.

- You routinely record new product ideas in the system.

- Many of the submitted features are rejected. Otherwise, you're culling them before you enter them.

- You can generate the last product version's "new feature" list by running a report from this system.

- Your stakeholders can easily check on feature status, and they get warm fuzzies because it matches their expectations.

Warning Signs

- No new features are being added.

- Everything is priority one.

- Features get added but never implemented.

- Irrelevant features are being added.

7 Use a Testing Harness

A *testing harness* is the tool or software toolkit you use to create and run your tests. The alternative is handcrafting stand-alone tests (or, simpler still, having no tests at all!). *testing harness*

If your tests aren't automated, then you can't run them with a script. You require a person to run your test suite, and that costs time and money. People also tend to do things slightly differently every time. Interactive testing is invaluable to your testing effort but so is a good suite of automated tests. A good test suite, like a good tester or developer, is worth its weight in gold. It can help keep your product in top shape, catch issues quickly and give your developers rapid feedback about the state of the product. We've never seen a practice that can introduce quality to a shop like a good suite of automated tests running inside a CI system.

> **TIP 9**
>
> Exercise your product—automate your tests

There are a lot of advantages to using an "off the shelf" test framework. The feature set, for instance, should be more comprehensive than anything you can create on your own. You should find many complementary products if you select a well-known framework. For example, many of the XUnit test harnesses have supporting products that can generate reports based on their output formats. A great example is MetaCheck,[13] an open-source tool that collects and formats the output of several code checkers. If you visit SourceForge.net and search on *JUnit*, you'll find dozens of projects that have extended or enhanced JUnit's basic functionality. When you use a standard framework, you get a lot of extras for free.

On the other hand, not having a standard, compatible testing framework across your shop means that you'll have a series of incompatible harnesses. (Ask three developers and two testers to solve one problem, and you'll get nine solutions.)

Unless you want everyone on your team solving the same problems over and over, constantly reinventing the wheel, you should have a common

---

[13]http://metacheck.sourceforge.net

Defect-Driven Testing

Defect-driven testing guides your test creation effort by targeting code areas that have had (or still have) defects. This simple and effective approach to creating tests looks at where the bugs in your product are *today*. Don't be concerned with historical problem areas; look at what the developers complained about over lunch today. What code are they tracing right now? Find the code that the developers are working in today and use it to create your automated tests.

Using defect driven testing, you'll quickly build a test suite that directly addresses the issues that the development teams are currently having. When an area of your code becomes unstable, this type of testing quickly "inoculates" the code and prevents the active defects from recurring. If a product area is stable, then it doesn't have the same urgent need for testing coverage. Given unlimited resources, we would all strive for 100 percent code coverage from our automated tests, but out here in the real world we need to apply our limited resources where they will do the most good.

framework everyone can use. In other words, everyone needs to use the same framework in order to most efficiently leverage your work. Choose one that is lightweight and flexible so that it can be adapted for a specific project's needs. It shouldn't be so rigid that it can't service multiple product lines.

Be sure it has a command-line interface so you can drive it from an external script or tool. It should also be able to handle a unit test, a product test, or an integration test.

TIP 10

Use a common, flexible test harness

There are many different kinds of testing; each one is targeted at identifying a different kind of problem.

Unit tests

Unit tests are designed to test your individual class or object. They are stand-alone, and generally require no other classes or objects to run. Their sole purpose in life is to validate the proper operation of the logic within a single unit of code.

Functional tests are written to test your entire product's proper operation (or function). These tests can address your entire product or a major subsystem within a product. They test many objects within the system.

Performance tests measure how fast your product (or a critical subsystem) can run. Without these tests, you can't tell whether a code change has improved or degraded your product's response time (unless you are really good with a stopwatch!).

Load tests simulate how your product would perform with a large load on it, either from a large number of clients or from a set of power users (or both!). Again, without this type of test, you can't objectively tell if your code base has been improved or degraded.

Smoke tests are lightweight tests and must be carefully written to exercise key portions of your product. You would use smoke tests because they run fast but still exercise a relevant portion of your product. The basic idea is to run your product to see if it "smokes," i.e., fails when you invoke basic functions. Smoke tests are very good to use with your CI system (see Practice 4, *Build Automatically*, on page 31) because they're fast. During your product's life cycle, the smoke tests that you actively run will probably rotate. Your smoke test suite targets areas of active development or known bugs.

Integration tests look at how the various pieces of your product lines work together. They can span many products: sometimes your products and sometimes the third-party products you use. For instance, various databases used by your product can be exercised as part of your integration tests. You want these tests to cross product boundaries. Integration tests are often used to validate new versions of the components your product depends on, such as databases. If a new version of your favorite database comes out, you will want to know if your product can run with it. A suite of tests that exercise functionality all the way down to the database should answer the question of functionality for you and also give you a quick look at your performance with the new components.

Mock client testing is used to create tests from your client's point of view. A mock client test tries to reproduce common usage scenarios for your product, ensuring that the product meets minimum functional specifications. This type of testing can be very effective for getting essential testing coverage in place to cover the most commonly used code paths. Also see the sidebar on the following page.

Functional tests

Performance tests

Load tests

Smoke tests

Integration tests

Mock client testing

Mock Client Testing

Mock client testing is a concept we developed that's catching on fast. Consider how your product will be used. It can be used by client applications (if you're developing a product) or by lower-level code (if you're writing an API). Write a test suite that emulates the client's behavior. A mock client test uses your product (or a subsystem) just like a normal client would. You have "mocked up" a client, just like a Mock Object* imitates a server or application resource. These are usually categorized as integration tests because they can be run against live systems. They can be chained together into performance and load tests, or individually they can be used as smoke tests. The concept is quite flexible and powerful! If you have a set of user scenarios, you can put them into a Mock Client Test and verify that they run (and continue to run after you refactor the code base!).

Using mock client tests, you exercise the most important code paths in your system: the ones the running code will invoke. It may not give you the percent of code coverage that other test methodologies will, but they get you the coverage that matters the most. Mock client tests are especially important in shops where testing resources are at a premium.

When you look at all the types of tests, mock client tests give you the best return on your investment. If you're responsible for a project that has no tests, start here and add the other types of tests later. Combining mock client tests with a defect driven test (see the sidebar on page 44) strategy will ensure that the code areas that need the most attention get test coverage in the most efficient manner.

*See http://www.mockobjects.com/Faq.html.

Don't get trapped by a bad testing framework. Make sure you have a very flexible product. Tomorrow, you may need to test something very different from today's product. If you have a flexible product, you will be able to just pick it up and continue working. If you have an overly specialized or rigid framework, you'll have to find another toolkit and start learning it from scratch. *Time is your most precious resource.* Don't waste it learning nonreusable tools.

At a rather large company we saw a great example of defect-driven testing combined with mock client testing. Over lunch we heard developers complaining about a specific bit of code in the bowels of their product that had broken three times in the last week. The problems were serious enough to make their entire product blow up, and the team spent nearly a day locating the problem. When the problem was fixed the first time, a second related problem was introduced. It took half a day to isolate that problem. Then, when fixing the second problem, the first problem was reintroduced. This time they located it in a just a few hours. The entire software team was involved each time; they were at a standstill. They couldn't do any other work. We did a rough calculation and found that the team had wasted two man months dealing with this problem.

After hearing about the recurring issue from the lunch crowd, we redirected the testers who were working in this area. They created tests from the point of view of the upper-level code (a client of the problematic lower-level code) and wrote the tests to specifically expose the bugs from the previous week. It took one tester only half a day to get the basic test in place; sample code was provided by the developers who had spent lots of time debugging the problem and already had the issue well-defined.

We then added the test to a CI system that ran the tests every time a developer added or changed code. The following week, someone reintroduced the old, defective version of the code twice. Now that the CI system was running these new tests, it caught the issue within a half-hour of the new code being checked in. The problem was fixed and verified (by the automated tests) within an hour. Without the CI system and the new test, the problem would have slipped back into the product and caused the same problems yet again.

The tests were written from the point of view of the client (the upper-level code), which is the underlying principle of mock client tests. The test functionality was identified by a recent bug—that's how defect-

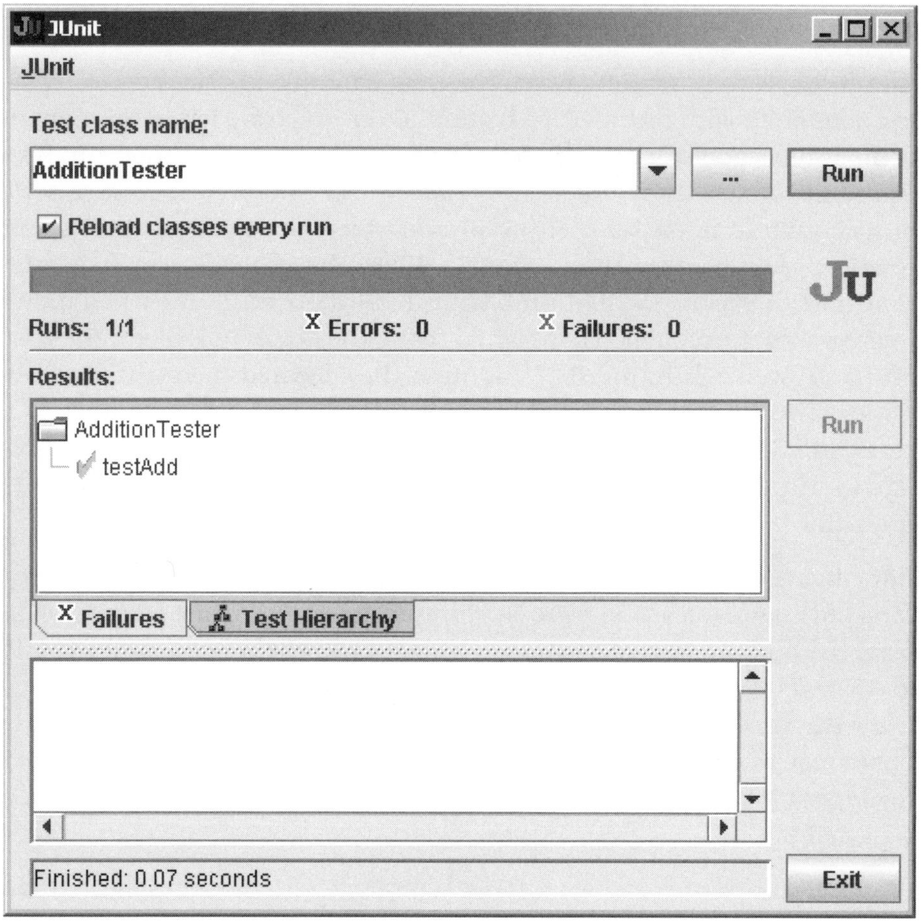

Figure 2.6: JUNIT CONSOLE, SHOWING ALL-TESTS-PASS

driven testing works. By applying these two powerful principles, you can take existing test resources and multiply their effectiveness.

Here's an example of JUnit test code (the GUI showing the test passing is show in Figure 2.6 on the facing page).

```
import junit.framework.*;
public class AdditionTester extends TestCase {
    public void testAdd() {
        assertEquals(5, 2 + 3);
    }
    public static void main (String[] args) {
        junit.swingui.TestRunner.run(AdditionTester.class);
    }
}
```

A good testing framework can have an incredible impact on your development effort. It can be a powerful tool when used effectively. Be sure that you invest the time to find a framework that's appropriate for your environment and then learn how to use it effectively.

How Do I Get Started?

If your team has no tests at all, you may want to discuss it with your tech lead (or manager). You can add tests to your areas of responsibility to show the benefit, but for maximum benefit the entire team should participate as well.

If your team is already writing tests, find out what they're using for a framework. Many developers write their own framework—don't go there! But if anyone in your shop has settled on a standard framework or tool, find out what it is and why they selected it; leverage their experience and expertise.

Once you've selected a framework, use the defect-driven strategy to create tests for your code. We strongly suggest you create mock client tests, and that you run all your tests in a CI system. A CI system is the best way to assure the tests are run regularly.

1. Select a testing tool or toolkit.
2. Start adding tests to problem areas.
3. Ensure that your tests are being run in an automatic build system (see Practice 4, *Build Automatically*, on page 31).

Am I Doing This Right?

Your answers to these questions will make it clear if you're on the right path:

> ### Don't Know Much About History
>
> Code with historical issues doesn't always indicate a poor developer. There are many reasons for code to fall into this category. Perhaps the code is very intricate, or there were multiple developers in the same area, and their work has been colliding. A new developer may have taken over for another colleague and was transitioning into the new area.
>
> Don't assume code with a high number of bugs was written by poor developers. Assume instead that the problems being solved were difficult. You will be able to create very effective tests once you identify those complexities.

- Is your test suite effective? Are your tests catching bugs?

- What are your code coverage[14] numbers? Are they increasing over time?

- Is the product you're testing stable?

- Are the tests being run automatically?

- Do your tests tell you whether they pass or fail? (If you have to manually determine whether they passed or failed, they aren't automated.)

- Does everyone in your shop have the ability to add tests? (If not, the framework is probably too complicated.)

Warning Signs

Have another look at your strategy if your tests:

- Aren't being run

- Never catch any problems

- Take too long to run

- Require significant effort to maintain

---

[14] *Code coverage* refers to the number of lines of code that are exercised by the tests you run.

8 On Choosing Tools

If you don't have a specific tool for each category we discuss, have a second look. For example, never bundle your build system with your IDE. You can do nearly anything with today's most popular IDEs. They slice, dice, and even julienne your code for you. Sure, these all-purpose tools do many things adequately, but they do nothing exceptionally well.

Invest time evaluating tools that fit your needs rather than using a bundled afterthought that doesn't quite do what you want. Don't compromise on the tools you use. You can choose from a broad range of commercial or open-source products for any tool you need. Every tool you use should be the best one for the job; shoot for the "best of breed" in each area.

Be sure your tools use an open format like XML or plain text. Use a tool that reads and writes in an open format so it "talks" with any other tool that uses open formats (assuming that semantics match or can be transformed to match). This adaptability lets you chain various tools together to form a complete end-to-end system. There's an amazing level of synergy you can get out of this type of interaction between seemingly unrelated tools.

> **Tip 11**
>
> Use the best tool for the job

You can see a great example of this concept in the open-source Java build tool Maven. Maven encapsulates your build process by using Ant scripts and Jelly, an Ant scripting language. Your tests are run automatically (Maven can drive the JUnit testing framework), and then Maven transforms your test results into HTML reports. Your reports range from raw test results to code coverage to static code analysis. You can use Maven to chain these tools together because they all use open formats as their input and output. Maven simply pipes the information around. You can see the point even though this short description grossly oversimplifies what Maven does. You can chain your tools together only if they read and write open formats.

As a counterexample, look at a format called Electronic Design Interchange Format (EDIF). Almost all early programs that used the format had a nice import utility that let you read data in EDIF. However, none of them would let you export data in EDIF, making it easy for you to migrate away from the competition but impossible to leave a vendor once they had your data. This "feature set" also made it nearly impossible for you (or any third party) to write tools to complement these systems. This inadequacy completely defeated the purpose of EDIF. Be sure the tools you use read *and* write open formats. Don't let vendors "EDIF" you.

TIP 12

Use open formats to integrate tools

---

9 ▶ When Not to Experiment

Never have a vital part of your product cycle (such as the build system) written in a niche or noncore technology, especially if only one developer knows it. Use a technology that anyone in the shop can configure and maintain. Technology playgrounds are fine, and necessary for professional development, but this isn't the place for them. Experiments must exist outside of the critical path.[15]

In one startup, the build script had been written in a new language; it was a learning project for the developer who wrote it. Worse, it was a general-purpose scripting language, not a build system. It contained more than 25 pages of spaghetti code that used every possible obscure language feature. Needless to say, the code was incomprehensible. It featured hard-coded dependencies on one developer's machine, on specifically setup network drives, and on specific versions of software components. The program was just a mess.

Never let a critical technology (like your build system) be created as a technology experiment. Use a tool designed for builds to create your builds, not the cool new technology that a team member wants to learn. There are plenty of noncritical areas for technology learning to take place. Never create automated tools that run on only one machine. Never hard-code network drive dependencies. Put everything you need in your SCM system, and the network drives become unimportant.

For example, if you are working in a Java shop, consider using Ant as your build script. Ant's whole purpose in life is to build Java programs, so it's a lot easier to write Java build scripts in Ant than in a language such as Python. Python is a great language, but it doesn't know anything about Java. Leverage your existing expertise when selecting your build system.

You gain a lot by adhering to this rule; it makes maintenance of the tool much easier. Anyone in the shop will be able to work with the technology and make adjustments. Also, by requiring experience, you avoid getting caught by a technology that looks great for a given situation but actually isn't.

---

[15]Your project's *critical path* contains anything that can slow down your project. Your SCM system and build scripts are good examples of items in your critical path. When they break, everything else stops as well.

But This Stuff Is Sooo Cool!

If you think a certain technology should be the exception to the rule (never make core technologies an experiment), then spend the time and money to get everyone trained. Don't just bring in the new technology and assume it's so great that everyone will learn it. It never happens that way. Use feedback to make sure people learn what you expect them to learn. Remember that such feedback reflects the talent of the teacher, not the stupidity of the student.

Only experience can tell you about a given technology's shortcomings.

One other danger worth mentioning involves letting any code wizard (or build script) do anything for you that you don't understand yourself. It's fine to let a tool handle details for you, but only if you already understand those details. If you don't, you'll be completely lost when something breaks. "Don't use wizard code you don't understand" [HT00].

TIP 13

Keep critical path technologies familiar

Never confuse activity with
progress.
► Author unknown

Chapter 3

Pragmatic Project Techniques

Why is it that some projects produce quality software on or ahead of schedule, while others (many others, unfortunately) end up late, over budget, or cancelled entirely? There are many ideas about why this happens, and many methodologies to fix it. One of the cornerstones of these methods is improving *collaboration*.

collaboration

Unless you're developing code in your garage, you're going to be working with other people. And even if you *are* working on a project at home, your customer is paying you to write it. Most of us work on software development teams. We work with our fellow team members, collaborating on the software product we're developing.

Though good collaboration doesn't guarantee a project's success, poor collaboration almost always guarantees a project's failure.

In this chapter we'll present some collaborative techniques we use to keep projects running smoothly and productively. You'll become more aware of your project's status, as well as your team members' progress by using these ideas. These techniques make your work easier, more productive, and more fun.

There is no canonical list of project-improving techniques. Each project and each team is different, and the state of the art is always advancing in both software development and in understanding good group dynamics.

As you move through your career, you will always have one more trick to learn and one more habit to drop when it is no longer relevant. The techniques we describe here are the ones we find the most useful. They include the following:

- The List

- The tech lead

- Daily meetings

- Code reviews

- Code change notifications

You might remember these practices as part of the larger figure on page 5, shown here by themselves.

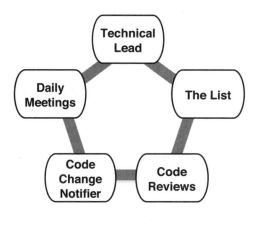

Figure 3.1: PROJECT TECHNIQUES

10 ▶ Work from The List

Many times we use a to-do list to track our work. The List formalizes the to-do concept so we can use it in a team setting.

In the past, when working on smaller projects, we used legal pads and notebooks to track our work. The List began as our personal to-do list of things we didn't want to forget. As we transitioned into more leadership roles, The List we were using began to contain teamwide items and paper became inefficient. After you show other team members The List enough times, you start looking for alternative ways to record and share The List. A white board works fine for a small group, especially in a large room with cubes (can you say *startup*?). These days we tend to use web pages or wikis. Some people use a spreadsheet[1] for The List. Everyone can access a web page, and it's easy to edit as well.

The List is how you set your daily and weekly agendas. You order your work with The List, as does the entire team (it's fractal!). When you get swamped, overwhelmed, or scattered, you come back to The List and use it to regain your focus. If you get stuck on a tough problem and you need to step away for a while, The List gives you a readily available set of items to use as filler. This ensures that you're working on the most important item, rather than the proverbial "squeaky wheel."

Why You Need The List

How often have you worked on a project where everyone was staying busy but the product was never complete? Important features were forgotten, team members were held up waiting for features that weren't done, and developers were stuck, not knowing what to work on next.

Someone needs to write down all the features, sort them by priority, and let team members grab their next job from the top of The List. You create a central point of organization for your team without the overhead of most heavyweight processes.

Team members that have The List never run out of work. When they finish their current task, they check out The List, pick a feature within the top-priority items, and go to work. Developers can pick their next

---

[1]Joel Spolsky uses an Excel spreadsheet to track his work list, and he has a lot of good reasons that you should also use something just as simple. See http://www.joelonsoftware.com/articles/fog0000000245.html

Joe Asks...

What's a Wiki?

A *wiki* is an easy way for people to create web pages. Wiki pages are written in a simple markup, not HTML, so anyone can add content. Wikis are designed to encourage group collaboration.

A Wiki page looks like any other web page initially, except that there's an "edit this page" link at the bottom. Clicking on that link puts the content of the current page in a simple HTML text edit box, so you can make changes to the page very easily.

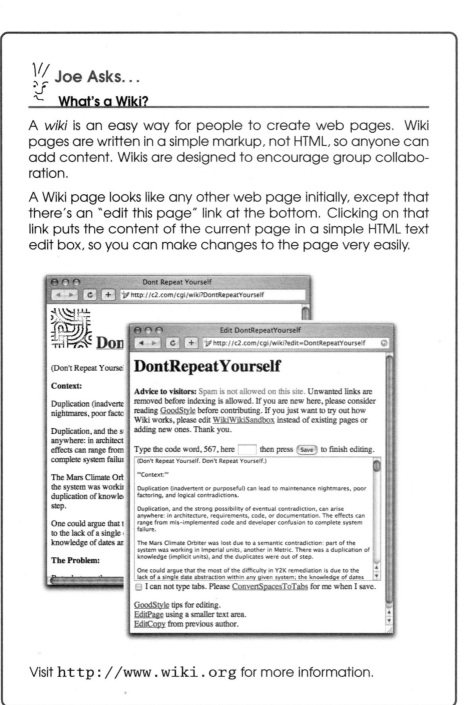

Visit http://www.wiki.org for more information.

job so they can still pick the work that is most interesting to them, but the tech lead knows that the features that are the highest priority are in progress or next on The List.

Since all developers are at different skill levels, the tech lead makes exceptions as needed, but generally, no second-priority item can be touched until the first-priority items are complete.

The List (as a team tool) gives management and customers something concrete to look at and evaluate the product before the time is invested adding the features. It's always cheaper to remove a feature before you've spent a week adding it! How many times have you finished a product and then had the customer say, "The product is okay, but I would have really loved it if you had put in feature A instead of X, Y and Z"? You create a piece of lightweight documentation that you can show people early in the development cycle when you use The List.

The List also provides a great deal of agility to your team. The List assures that you've done some basic design work up front by ensuring that you've decomposed your product into features and features into list items, as needed. Also, because your product is separated into features, you can drop out items or add others as needed.

Most companies have an individual or two who will rush in and demand to know why feature X was not finished or is not being worked on. (Their viewpoint: isn't the feature that I care about the most important one?) With a defined and prioritized set of tasks in hand, you can show them what features you're developing and why they are more important to the core product. This explanation is usually enough to satisfy the person and show them that you're doing useful work.

Your comprehensive list of features with priorities that make sense is a confidence builder for the team, for management, and for other teams that might depend on your efforts. Having The List several items deep demonstrates you are thinking ahead and planning your next steps.

TIP 14

Work to The List

How Should I Use The List?

You can use The List for your own work or for your entire team. Either way is easy and very effective. We use it both ways.

The List As an Organizational Tool

Through the years we've worked in a variety of roles, but we've rarely worn a single hat. As a general rule we, like most people, end up with lots of different jobs to do and very little time to get them done. When we try to juggle all the work in our heads, we tend to spread our time so thin on a lot of tasks and end up getting no substantial work done.

Our solution is to use The List as a personal organizer as well. While we always use the group list for the entire team, we've found that having our own copy of what we have to do is very helpful. Make a list each morning of what is on your plate and then prioritize it. At the end of the day, review what you did (or didn't) finish. Decide if you didn't get everything done because you were overly optimistic about what you thought you could get done or because you were distracted during the day. For a more complete discussion of using your own list to order your personal work list, get a copy of *The Seven Habits of Highly Effective People* by Stephen Covey.

Getting started with your own copy of The List is easy. First, create a list of every task you are working on (or have pending). Then, with your tech lead, assign a priority to each item. Finally, put a time estimate with each item. Don't worry about getting the time estimates perfect the first time, you'll improve over time.

Getting your team started on The List isn't hard either if your product is already well-defined. It's actually a great group activity that can help the entire team understand the project's overall direction.

1. Put every feature that you are adding to your project on a white board. This can take a while and often takes more than one white board.
2. Assign priorities to each feature. Be sure to include the proper stakeholders (management, customers, etc.) in this process. It's ideal to have your entire team in on the process, but if you have strongly opinionated team members, it may be smoother to just include the tech lead and the stakeholders.
3. Rewrite all of the features, sorted by priority.
4. Attach time estimates to each item.

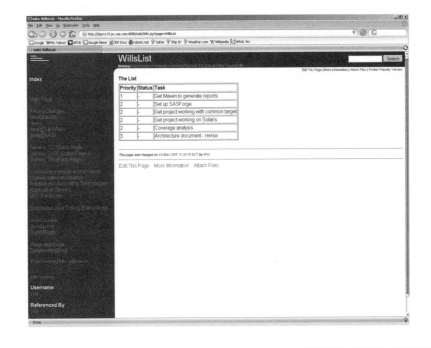

Figure 3.2: THE LIST ON AN INTRANET WEB PAGE

Until the current top priority items are completed, no one can work on the lower-priority items. This ensures that all the priority-one items are in progress before any of the priority-two tasks are touched.

As you can see, getting started using The List is fairly easy. However, to be effective, The List must adhere to a number of rules. It must be all of the following:

- Publicly available

- Prioritized

- On a time line

- Living

- Measurable

- Targeted

Next we'll look at what each of these rules means, and what it means to us and our team.

\\// **Joe Asks...**
 ○ ○
  ~   <u>**What's RSS?**</u>

Depending on who you ask, RSS stands for either "Rich Site Summary" or "Really Simple Syndication" or "RDF Site Summary." It's a way of sharing changes to content. It's very popular with web sites with dynamic content (like news sites or build status). When a web site shares their changes using RSS, it's called an *RSS feed*. An RSS feed is an XML file that lists changes or new content.

An *RSS reader* is a program that checks on all the RSS feeds you've subscribed to and shows you the new stuff. RSS feeds are made available on web servers, so an RSS reader is really just looking at a file on a web site and showing you the changes.

RSS readers are a really convenient way to get your news in a digest format. They collect news until you are ready to read it.

Publicly Available

Your team's List must be publicly available. A secret list doesn't help collaboration. Put The List on your white board or web site, make an RSS feed for it, or otherwise make it very easy and obvious for people to read. Keeping The List in front of you helps you maintain your focus. It gives you an easy review of pending work that you can scan quickly—especially when you're scattered or distracted during a hectic day. Keeping it publicly visible helps your manager keep track as well.

Prioritized

The List must be prioritized. It's very important to recognize the different types of features involved in a product: necessary features, desired features, and fluff features. You *must* make these distinctions when prioritizing The List, or you will be wasting your time. There will always be a core set of tasks that must be accomplished before the product can ship; these are the top-priority features. For instance, these might include the login screen, the installer, or a working database. You simply cannot ship your product without them. Having a new and

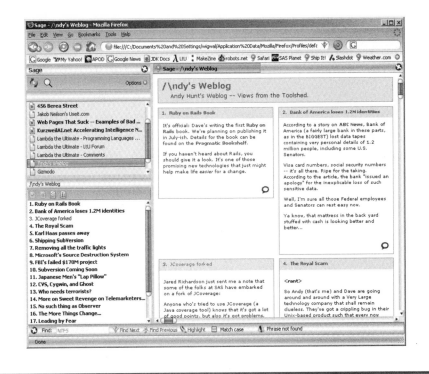

Figure 3.3: AN RSS NEWSREADER

improved background color for the About dialog box would probably be considered a fluff feature.

Never, ever, bypass the priorities you've set. Finish all the higher-priority items before working on lower-priority items, unless there's a *good*—and widely publicized—reason to temporarily put one on hold.

Time Estimates

The List always has a time line associated with it. The time line should not be set in stone, but it should include estimates for how long each item on the list should take to complete. Then, as you complete an item, record how long it actually took and pay attention to the difference.

Over time, you—and everyone on the team—will get very good at estimating how long a given task will take. After a few iterations, the tech lead should be able to create rough project time lines based on individual team member's lists, and the project manager should be able to do the same thing. *There are no wrong answers when estimating.* Some estimates will be closer than others. Don't worry about how much you miss an estimate at first. Like a muscle, this skill grows as you use it.[2]

Living

To be effective, it must be a living list. Your team must be able to adapt to change. The tech lead will adjust feature priorities as the project progresses; new features will appear while others fade away. Priorities change. This is a Good Thing! It can be frustrating until you get used to it, but remember that your company is trying to be competitive in a changing marketplace. They depend on you to be flexible as well. Instead of fighting it, work with it.

In fact, changes to The List usually mean that your customers and stakeholders are looking at the project and are actually giving mind share—and valuable feedback—to it. Most customers wait until the project is finished to look at your work, but by then it's too late. It's always better to get feedback earlier, even if it might be frustrating to see The List frequently change. If The List hasn't evolved in a while, it probably doesn't reflect the current priorities of the project.

Measurable

In order to be effective, every item on The List must be measurable. After all, you must be able to determine whether the item is done if you want to mark it off your list.

This criteria eliminates vague items like "performance improvements" but encourages "Make login complete in less than five seconds" or "Generate report X in less than ten seconds." By creating a goal with a binary state, you make it possible to tell when it's done. An open-ended goal like "performance improvements" can last the life of the product and end up being a black hole.

If you currently have items on The List that are not measurable, take the time to look at what the real requirement is. Did the item come from a request for faster reporting or faster startup times? Break down the item into defined, binary items, and then get the person who asked

---

[2]If your team is having trouble with estimates, try to limit the choices; for instance, every estimate must be one day, one week, two weeks, or four weeks. Allow no other choices at first.

Feature-Boxed Iterations Instead of Time-Boxed Iterations

The problem with time-boxing is that we ship product features, not calendar days, to our customers.

When your team is using The List, and all the items are ordered by their priority, your releases become feature boxed, not time boxed. Management can look at the The List and draw a line beneath the features that they need in the next release. You then add up the time estimates for those features and calculate the release date. Your individual product and industry will dictate how long to schedule for your internal testing and beta programs, but you can concretely schedule your development *code freeze*.

When your sales team decides that a given feature must be included, that feature's priority on The List can change, and it can migrate into the shipping features. However, the time associated with the feature *must* be added to the ship date.

This way of working gives your sales force and management team a clear and defined way to understand the trade-off between specific features and time. They are no longer trying to make decisions about ship dates and features in a vacuum. Instead of trying to abstractly weigh features that take more time, they are weighing two specific features, with specific time frames.

We feel that this approach gives you the product when it's ready, as soon as it can be ready, instead of letting your company dictate an arbitrary release date that you miss. Our industry is famous for missing deadlines, and no wonder given the way we write software. Instead of trying to push an arbitrary feature set into an arbitrary deadline, companies should let their development team tell them what they can do! If the developers can't hit the mark that sales wants, is it better to find out now and adjust your plans or find out later, when you miss the deadline? And if the development team can hit the mark *early*, wouldn't it be nice to know so that the company can add features to the release or get it out the door to customers sooner?

The first time you release a product this way, management will be nervous. The second time, they'll be relaxed. The third time, management will have learned to trust their software teams to deliver what they promised!

\\// Joe Asks...
~;f
~ __What's a Code Freeze?__

A *code freeze* is when your code base stops changing. During your development cycle, code is fluid, like water, and changes constantly. However, after the code freezes, the changes stop. Only major bug fixes can be made after a code freeze. Feature additions and minor bug fixes are not allowed.

Oftentimes a "code freeze" degrades into more of a "code slush" as ill-considered changes seep into the release.

for the original item to look at the items. This review will make sure that you are actually addressing the customer's need.

If an item can't be translated into measurable goals, then bump it to the lowest priority and get working on the higher-priority items. Removing the item entirely can be a mistake if the original idea for the item was a good one; it simply needs to be boiled down to the measurable pieces.

Targeted

You've probably noticed by now that we have talked about both team lists and individual lists. Each type of list is very important and must be targeted at the proper audience. The List for your team will be a lot larger and have all the outstanding work for the entire project on it. Your individual version of The List will contain fewer team items (sometimes only a single item for the project), but as soon as you are done, you copy an item from the team's list and put it on yours.

Although it is very simple, The List is a powerful tool on many levels. It keeps you organized and on-track and keeps your management chain informed and involved in your work direction. Creating and prioritizing The List makes you think through your work and map out your next steps. Any great pool player will tell you that they have their next eight shots planned out; so will any great developer!

Your List Looks Like This

Here is an example of what your personal list might look like, sorted by priority:

1. Add a new report that displays widgets produced per day.

2. Add a new report that displays widgets produced per employee.

3. Look at bug #12345 (widgets per month shows zero when viewing five-month report).

4. Install development tools on my new workstation.

5. Check out cool new WhatChaMuhCallIt-Reports... might make a good addition to the next edition's report system.

Notice that the most important items are at the top. In this case the new features are more important than the bug fix, but that's not always the case. Also, the computer upgrade and research project are at the bottom of the list. These items are for filler when you get some down-time (perhaps you are waiting on someone else?) or you need a break. It's important to have the filler items on the list so that lower-priority items don't get forgotten.

How to Get Started

1. For an entire day, write down every task as you work on it (this will be your "finished" list).

2. Organize whatever daily task list you do have into a formal copy of The List.

3. Ask your tech lead to help you prioritize your work and add rough time estimates.

4. Start working on the highest-priority item on The List—no cheating! If some crisis forces a lower-priority item higher, record it.

5. Add all new work to The List.

6. Move items to your finished list as you complete tasks (this makes surviving status reports and "witch-hunts" much easier).

The act of creating The List forces you to organize and prioritize your work. Just as keeping a diary helps you think through and understand what you've been doing, The List helps you sort out your current workload but in a fairly high-level, lightweight way.

Review The List every morning. Update it whenever new work pops up. . . especially the last-minute crisis tasks; you're likely to forget about those when someone asks you what you on earth you did all last week.

You're Doing It Right If...

- Is every one of your current tasks on The List?

- Does The List accurately portray your current task list?

- Did the tech lead or customer help you to prioritize The List?

- Is The List publicly available (electronically or otherwise)?

- Do you use The List to decide what to work on next?

- Can you update (and publish) The List quickly?

Warning Signs

- You fail to add tasks to The List because you're "too busy."

- More time is spent updating The List than completing the tasks.

- It takes weeks for team members to complete individual items on their personal lists (hint: the items are too big).

- The List is updated less than once a week.

- Priorities on The List don't match "real" priorities.

- The List is a closely held secret, not visible to anyone outside your team.

- In addition to the team's list, there are other publicly available versions that differ.

ʬ Joe Asks...

What If My Team Won't Use The List?

Even if your entire team doesn't use The List, you can use it personally. Write it on your white board or a legal pad, on a wiki on your PDA, or on your own web page. Ask your tech lead for help in prioritizing the items on it, and use their feedback to order your work. Check items off as you complete them, and reevaluate The List weekly. Using The List this way will be just as effective for your personal use as it could be for your entire team. Eventually a good tech lead will notice your use of The List and begin using it for the entire team. You'll be surprised at how often good habits spread. It may take a while, but people notice what works.

▶ 11 A Tech Leads

Your *tech lead* both oversees and carries the technical responsibility   *tech lead*
for your software project. Having a tech lead frees up your manager
to handle bureaucratic matters while delegating the technical aspects
to someone who's better equipped. Your manager may double as the
tech lead, but this isn't required and in many cases just isn't a good
idea. Having a separate tech lead is ideal when your manager lacks
the required technical expertise or when your teams are working on
multiple projects.

Why You Need a Tech Lead

Have you ever worked for a manager who didn't understand the technology you were using? They set unrealistic deadlines, don't understand delays, and argue about time lines. All this happens because they don't understand what you're doing or how the technology works. It's difficult for someone who has never worked as a developer to understand your work. While it may be okay for someone in sales to know only how to use your product, your tech lead must understand exactly how it works. The person who is responsible for scheduling features and mapping out development work must understand what the code is doing to be effective. What you need is a technically savvy liaison to explain the product and technologies to nontechnical managers. You need a person to be the interface between the development team and management. You need a tech lead.

Usually the tech lead is a team member who moves into a leadership role. They understand the technical problems the team is facing because of their development background. They don't commit to insane deadlines because they understand what a "simple" feature request actually requires. Your tech lead can eliminate, or at least minimize, the meddling of nontechnical management.

At one end of the spectrum you've got the nontechnical manager, and at the other side is the manager who stays holed up all day writing code and doesn't interface with management or customers. This manager is a stereotypical developer who hides in their office avoiding the nontechnical world. Your team builds products that nobody wants, and your priorities are based on your manager's whims rather than the customer's needs. Time after time your team builds products that are shelved. Upper management doesn't know what your team is doing, so they assume you're doing nothing, which ruins your chances for bonuses, raises, and promotions. Your team needs an advocate who takes the time to create reports and give presentations to management, customers, and anyone else whose perception of your project matters. Here again, you need a tech lead.

Your tech lead lives with a foot in both worlds. They must work with and understand the development team and also meet with management, customers, and other tech leads to communicate what your team is doing. By taking the time to meet with and understand your product's customers, they're in a unique position to understand what your product should do.

You need a tech lead to do the following:

- Make sure your team's work priorities are in line with customer needs

- Ensure that your team's work is properly represented to management

- Insulate your team from nontechnical upper management

- Relay technical issues to nontechnical stakeholders

- Present nontechnical concerns to the development team

Joe Asks. . .

What's a Stakeholder?

A *stakeholder* is someone who has a stake in your product. When you are working on a product, it's important to identify who your audience will be. Your customers might be your stakeholders, but if you haven't identified them yet, the sales (or marketing) crew can stand in. At small companies your investors are often your stakeholders. Sometimes in larger companies your stakeholders are other departments who build their products on top of yours. It's important to identify these key people so you can build the product that they need.

So what must a tech lead do in order to accomplish this laundry list of tasks?

The Responsibilities of the Tech Lead

The tech lead has several major areas of responsibility that will vary by company and team composition. The following is a minimal list of a tech lead's responsibilities:

- Set direction for team members.

- Orchestrate your project's feature list.

- Prioritize your project's features.

- Insulate your team from external distractions[3].

Let's take a closer look at each of these responsibilities.

Set Direction for Team Members

The tech lead is your team's director, setting direction and priority. The tech lead works with each team member to create and maintain a personal copy of The List (see Practice 10, *Work from The List*, on page 57). Tech leads use their knowledge of team members' progress, problems, and estimated completion dates to build a big-picture view of

---

[3]There is risk of overdoing it, though: overinsulation will filter out valuable feedback as well.

your project's health and to track progress. This single point of contact provides a quick way for anyone to get accurate status updates on your project.

Manage the Project's Feature List

The tech lead acts as the master keeper of the feature list for your project. Rather than have feature requests drop in developers' laps, all feature requests are filtered through the tech lead. They manage all feature changes.

The tech leads are placed in a unique position to understand not only the technical ramifications of each feature but also the desires and wishes of the project's stakeholders. The tech lead adds and removes project features as needed and guides the efforts of your team.

The tech lead and stakeholders first establish the scope of work by creating a list of features (The List is a great way to do this!). Then the tech lead meets with the entire team to estimate the time for each feature. Sometimes this means breaking a big feature down into several list items. Finally, the tech lead assigns corresponding tasks to individual developers for implementation and establishes rough project time lines (note that the estimates will be revised as the project progresses, but more on that later).

Having the tech lead manage your project's feature list really helps when you have people constantly trying to add extra features to your project. A tech lead acts as a buffer, filtering the requests and getting a reasonable priority on each request.

A tech lead can be very useful in running interference for your team. For example, most companies have a few overly "creative" types. These people always have great ideas for your product, but their ideas are usually distractions for your team. This type of person always seems to drop in when you are at your busiest.

One particularly creative executive we worked with, Ernest, was worse than most. To mitigate his impact, we had him bring his ideas to us (instead of team members), and we would add his new feature idea to the team's copy of The List (which we kept on a white board). After adding the feature, we would compare it to the priority-one features (the required features), and we would all agree it wasn't one of those. Then we would compare it to the priority twos, and so on. The new feature would always end up as a priority five, a very much optional, fluff feature.

Eventually Ernest learned our system and began adding his features to the bottom of the white board, below the priority fives. Because he added them to The List, the features were not forgotten. Some were actually added to our product, but they always ended up in the next release, not the current one. By handling the creative personalities this way, your Ernests get their input into the system, but your team doesn't get interrupted with new ideas or waste time adding fluff features.

Assign Priorities to Each Feature

You need to set an order for your new list. Without an established order, everyone might just select the interesting features and neglect the necessary ones. Getting the correct priority on each of your features is almost as important as having the right features on The List! Fortunately, this is a problem you can lay at your tech lead's feet. The tech lead must work with the project's stakeholders to set feature priorities.

Your stakeholders have a lot of influence on feature priority, and they always have a significant interest in the project and its success. However, your stakeholders usually don't have the technical background needed to make good decisions. They often just don't know what is technically possible or practical.

Your tech lead works with your stakeholders to set feature priority. Your tech lead can do this because he knows the capabilities of your team (a notion that gets continually refined based on real-world feedback) and he also knows the technical details of the project.

During this process, your tech lead will learn the nontechnical reasons stakeholders are asking for a feature. The tech lead and stakeholder work together and compromise to set feature priorities. This cooperation helps balance out a stakeholder with no technical experience or a tech lead with no customer experience.

In practice, the tech lead doesn't have to meet with the stakeholder to iron out every detail once both of them learn to understand and trust each other.

Insulate the Team from External Distractions

You're in the middle of an intricate project. You've been "in the groove" all morning, making wonderful progress when one of the sales critters

Priorities

Priorities have associated numbers, with priority one being the highest priority and priority five being the lowest. You will, of course, adjust these numbers to suit your needs. We currently use one to five, but in other situations, we've used one to ten. What matters is the order, not the size of the numbers.

- Priority One: Required
  These are the features that you absolutely cannot ship without.
- Priority Two: Very Important
  You could ship the product without completing these items, but you probably won't.
- Priority Three: Nice to Have
  Given time, you will complete them, but these items never delay a ship date.
- Priority Four: Polish
  These items add a finished feel to your product.
- Priority Five: Fluff
  If you have time to add "fluff" features, then you are ahead of schedule and under budget.

scampers in to ask a question about the next release and completely blows your train of thought. Annoys you just to read the situation, doesn't it? It's not just you; everyone works better without interruptions. In fact, researchers say that up to 40 percent of your workday can be lost to interruptions.[4] That's like going home after working less than five hours! Scientists have even named the phenomenon: *cognitive overload*.[5] Knowing this, the tech lead must make every effort to keep the team working without interruptions. A great way to do this is to use the tech lead as the point of contact for the developers. Always let the tech lead buffer the interruptions, whether they are from the IT staff or the stakeholders.

cognitive overload

---

[4]Researchers have confirmed that making someone *context switch* can have a profound impact on their productivity. The cost is between 20 and 40 percent. http://www.umich.edu/~bcalab/multitasking.html

[5]Dr. David Levy studies the ways multitasking affects our health and productivity in http://seattletimes.nwsource.com/pacificnw/2004/1128/cover.html.

Where Do The List Items Come From?

What sources can you use to gather features for The List? Can you use requirements documents? Requirement-level use cases? User stories? 3x5 cards? A large government contract? It doesn't matter. What matters is that you have features that can be put on The List and prioritized. The List doesn't replace your preferred method of gathering requirements. Instead, it takes information from every source and presents it in a clean, understandable format.

Again, to be perfectly clear, The List doesn't replace *how* you get your requirements. It replaces (or augments) their presentation to your team and co-workers.

What Does Your Tech Lead Look Like?

Tech leads split their time between development tasks and management tasks, not working exclusively in either realm. There will be days and even weeks when a tech lead will work in one area or the other, but most days will be split among both types of work.

Your tech lead is the gatekeeper of your project. Tech leads keep team members on-track and the feature list relevant. They also keep management informed of team progress and make sure the customer's point of view is represented. Your tech lead will look like a jack of all trades.

Naturally, the tech lead position can make or break a project (or their portion of it). It's not an easy job; it requires technical expertise, communication skills, and the ability to multitask.

Every project should have a good tech lead, and every developer should aspire to become one at least once. Even if you never take on the role, learning these skills will make you invaluable to your development group and your company. Most great technical talents have been a tech lead at least once in their careers.

> **Tip 15**
>
> Let a tech lead

How to Get Started

If you aspire to be a tech lead, you need to prove you're ready to handle the additional responsibility. Look over the job requirements, and strive to live up to them. Voluntarily perform as many of the tech lead duties as you can. Don't wait for the job to fall into your lap; demonstrate that you are trying to earn the position and can handle it well.

Use The List (see Practice 10, *Work from The List*, on page 57) for your personal work but also keep one for your team. Monitor work in progress while keeping an eye on upcoming projects.

Evaluate your team's process. Locating the weak spots and finding practices or concepts to address problems will give you a new perspective. For example, if your team is having trouble keeping the code compiling, then you should set up a CI system on your desktop (see Practice 4, *Build Automatically*, on page 31) to help solve the problem.

Don't give up if you aren't promoted to tech lead right away. Continue learning and growing for the next assignment. Not everyone has the temperament for a tech lead role, but working toward it gives you a broader picture of the entire project, which makes you a more productive team member. You become a better developer by thinking about and considering how you'd be a tech lead.

If you've just become a tech lead, create a rough road map. Chart where the team currently stands and the direction you want them to go. What problems will you address? What work will you encourage?

Make a list of all known problems. Then survey the team to see if they know about additional problems. When you think you've arrived at a real list, decide which items you can address and which you can't.

Daily meetings are a great way to keep track of your team's work without smothering them (see Practice 12, *Coordinate and Communicate Every Day*, on page 78).

You're Doing It Right If...

As your team's tech lead, you should be able to answer these questions favorably:

- Do you know what every member of your team is working on?

- Can you generate a project status summary in less than five minutes?

- What are the next five to ten features for your product?

- Can you readily list the highest-priority defects for your product?

- What was the most recent problem you cleared up for a team member?

- Would a team member come to you if they needed an important issue resolved?

Warning Signs

Here are some warning signs that your tech lead is ineffective or overbearing:

- Lacks big-picture view of every team member's work direction

- Causes work to halt when they show up

- Takes credit for the team's work

- Fails to solve problems, or worse, causes problems

- Inaccurately forecasts work time lines

- Is unaware of team members' technical proficiencies and/or what team members want to learn

- Is oblivious to personality clashes on the team

Coordinate and Communicate Every Day

The last thing most people want is more meetings. If your team meets weekly, each meeting is probably at least an hour with time spent discussing announcements, the last week's work, and the coming week's plans. Daily meetings are very different. They are brief team encounters that encourage interaction and communication without putting a huge dent in your schedule.

Each team member briefly shares what they are working on and what problems they've run into. A good rule of thumb is to spend no more than one to two minutes per person. Remember that this meeting has the entire team tied up, so be mindful of the burn rate; keep it short and to the point.

Why You Need Daily Meetings

The easiest way to address communication failures is to talk to your team more frequently. This will help you understand where there's a breakdown and then gives you a chance to fix it.

Most people try to work toward the team's goals. Unfortunately, people tend to misunderstand or lose direction, so you must take steps to adjust.

Meet more frequently with your entire team, and let everyone share what they are doing. The goal is to make frequent course corrections: if you want to steer a car down the road, you don't pick a direction and hold to it no matter what. You point the car where you want it to go, and then you make lots of very small corrections, turning the wheel left or right as needed. You'll run off the road and wreck the car if you wait too long to make a correction. Your software project will also crash if it goes too long without small corrections.

> TIP 16
>
> Use daily meetings for frequent course corrections

What the Daily Meeting Does for You

Daily meetings have a lot of benefits that you can start experiencing from the first day you have one.

Joe Asks...

What Is Burn Rate?

Burn rate is a term that describes how much money it costs to operate the company, including salaries, rent, electricity, benefits, and so on. It's the amount of money you "burn" whether you are getting work done or not. When you have meetings of any size, always step back and do a rough calculation of how much the meeting is costing you per hour. Knowing this number tends to keep meetings shorter.

As a good rule of thumb, assume that each developer costs $100 an hour (remember that we're counting overhead as well as direct salary). That means if you have ten people on your team, the ballpark burn rate is $1,000 an hour, $8,000 a day, and $40,000 a week. The next time you have a meeting that starts ten minutes late or everyone hears about Fred's vacation for thirty minutes, calculate the cost. When your product is three months late, how much did the development time cost your company? Remember that this example ignores the cost of lost opportunities during the wasted time.

Off-Track...Again

There are categories of developers that perpetually drift off course. The most common of these are the inexperienced developers and the tumbleweed developers. The new team members just don't know any better and will spend time solving problems that have already been solved. The tumbleweeds are older and more experienced, but they drift off course frequently. A daily meeting can help keep both types of people on-track.

Reinventing the Wheel

An inexperienced developer will solve problems that don't need solving. Bright young developers rarely encounter a problem they can't solve, but the problems they solve have usually already been solved by someone else. Unfortunately for these new graduates, team members usually don't talk enough to share this type of information. Instead of learning from the mistakes of their co-workers, new hires continue to reinvent the wheel, and the state of the art in computer science experiences much churn and little progress.

You'll recognize this problem when developers implement data structures provided by the language. These developers create nifty GUI widgets that duplicate what another developer wrote last month. Everyone in the shop ends up writing a personal copy of every utility you can think of. If everyone had been talking, the utilities could have been written once and shared by everyone. However, the developers in this shop have been too busy writing code to talk. Instead, every developer in the shop has GUI widgets with a slightly different look and feel and their own personal set of string manipulation routines.

When your team meets every day and your newest developer Lee tells everyone that he is starting a new set of GUI widgets, Ellen can tell him about the widgets that she and Mike worked on last year. The widgets might not be an exact fit for what Lee needs, but it's a starting point for his work. Instead of starting from scratch, Lee will build on the work already done by other team members. With a daily meeting, you have a forum for these types of discussions to take place instead of waiting until Lee happens to mention the GUI widgets to someone at lunch or in the break room.

Tumbleweed Developers

We've all worked with a few tumbleweed developers. These developers lose direction and drift through their days. They wade through random code and "improve" it, cleaning up method signatures, polishing algorithms, and reformatting brackets. Tumbleweed developers lack the discipline to finish any task you ask them to do and generally cause more harm than good.

One tumbleweed developer we know cleans up method signatures and removes unused arguments. For instance, in his hands

```
doSomething(String foo, Integer bar)
```

would become

```
doSomething(String foo)
```

Unfortunately, this developer, like most tumbleweeds, never changes the code that uses doSomething, so his changes often break builds.

Tumbleweed developers will retool your algorithms for speed, but their changes cause the code to generate wrong results. They'll spend hours reformatting code to suit their preferences. Tumbleweeds have a collection of habits that they practice because it's the "right thing" to do.

You can rein in a tumbleweed developer fairly easily. First, have daily team meetings. Second, pay attention to a tumbleweed's daily report. This is where a good tech lead will catch the wanderings before they go too far. Finally, your tech lead should be sure your tumbleweeds always have a full day's worth of work. This tactic doesn't eliminate the wandering completely, but it will minimize their free time your tumbleweeds have and limit their damage.

Expertise Multipliers

If you have a small number of senior members on your team, daily meetings leverage their expertise. Each time they share a solution, the entire team gets to hear it. On the other hand, each time a junior member talks about a problem, the senior members become aware of it and can help—if you aren't aware of the problem, you can't help solve it.

For example, say Ted comes to your daily meeting and says he is having problems getting an XML parser to handle international characters. Mike, who ran into the same problem last year, can tell Ted exactly how to solve this problem. Ted gets a quick answer to a problem instead of spending hours tracking the problem down by himself. Every team member can leverage the entire team's experience to solve problems quickly.

Team Communication

Daily meetings get everyone talking without putting any one person on the spot. Getting together daily to talk and share helps your team bond in an amazing way. How many teams do you know where every single member talks to every other member at least once a day? Daily meetings build your disconnected group of developers into a true team.

The type of developer who benefits the most from daily meetings is the one who is painfully shy and spends their days hiding in their office. One person we worked with (let's call him Rick) was the poster child for this personality type. Rick came in and went directly to his office, worked until lunch, which he ate alone in his office, and then left at the end of the day. Most days he did not even speak to another person.

Once the daily meetings started, all the team members—even Rick—got to know one another. Jokes flew before, during and after the meetings. Developers helped each other to solve problems. Camaraderie built up. The last we heard, Rick had completely emerged from his shell and was interacting with most of the team, asking people to lunch, dropping in "just to talk," and interacting on a level that, frankly, we didn't think possible.

We've seen this effect with lots of people at various starting points and always with positive results.

A Big-Picture Point of View

You prevent "my feature myopia" by meeting to discuss what other team members are working on. When this condition afflicts team members, they believe that their work is the only work and naturally the most important. This leads to all sorts of delusions of grandeur and gives developers quite an inflated opinion of their place in the world. Quite often just being in a group that is discussing the various projects and work directions can cure a person with no further treatments.

Beyond treating "my feature myopia," your entire team can benefit from knowing what other team members are doing. When Jeff and Mutt know that Jen is starting to refactor a component their code uses, they can plan to work in another code area so that Jen's work won't impact them. If Jen's refactoring is similar to work that Jeff has experience with, he can offer his help to her. You will see all sorts of beneficial side effects by sharing the information about what each team member is doing.

Alternatives

There are many alternatives to team meetings. Let's look at a few of them.

Your manager or tech lead can walk around and drop in on team members from time to time. This gives every team member one-on-one time with the tech lead and that's a good thing. However, it doesn't provide any teamwide interaction. It's also a huge waste of time for the tech lead who ends up spending a day or two each week walking around. Finally, instead of shielding the team from interruptions, your tech lead is now the one causing interruptions.

Another alternative is to leave everyone alone for a couple of months and then try to bring it all together at the end. While this remains a widely used option, we don't recommend it. It does lead to heroic efforts with lots of overtime at the end of the cycle, but it doesn't lead to many working products. When your team works in this much of a vacuum, miscommunications are magnified. If you get on the wrong track, you waste weeks or months before you realize it. We've worked in shops that operated this way and repeatedly seen months of developer's work thrown away.

Weekly meetings are also very popular. Our issue with weekly meetings is the volume of information that has to be shared to make a weekly meeting truly effective. Team members have done so much work in a week that it is impossible for any meaningful exchange of information to occur. Instead, weekly meetings become a forum for the manager to share information or announcements. A good manager can use this forum to focus the group on a particular issue or problem, but they can't focus on issues they don't know exist. Weekly meetings are better than quarterly, but it falls far short of what a daily meeting can do for your team.

Daily Meetings Look Like...

- 8:55 a.m.: Team members begin to drift into the meeting room. The meeting is a part of everyone's daily routine; it's held in the same room at the same time every day. The pre-meeting time is used to discuss vital issues, like which coffee shops have the best baristas, the latest in mountain bike technology, or cool homebrew MythTV projects.

- 9:00 a.m.: The tech lead, Maurice, calls the meeting to order. Some days this will mean having to interrupt various team members who are diligently discussing their new mountain bikes. A team member is tapped to give their status report, in this case, it starts with Chris.

  Chris worked on adding support for a new database to the product yesterday. He ran into a slight problem with some SQL syntax but got the problem isolated and fixed. Another team member chimes in with a tip about a few more SQL commands that also aren't portable. Now Chris knows someone else on his team who has ported SQL before and he has a resource up the hall he can ask questions.

- 9:03 a.m.: Tiffany is sitting beside Chris, so she talks next. Tiffany was writing a prototype client application that would potentially be a new front-end to the team's product. Tiffany spent the day coding the main screen for the application. She anticipates being finished with the GUI layout today and should begin adding the logic code behind the GUI after lunch.

- 9:04 a.m.: Mike was in the middle of a PC upgrade, and he spent the day reinstalling software and resetting preferences on that machine. Another fast report is completed.

- 9:05 a.m.: Fred is debugging a customer reported problem with the team's product. Apparently, the team's server product is regularly crashing on Monday mornings but runs fine the rest of the week. Jake jumps in with a story about another product he worked on with a similar issue. In that case, the database server was being rebooted over the weekend, and the product was crashing when his application tried to access it again on Monday morning. Jake proceeds to tell everyone the entire story. After several minutes Maurice interrupts and ends the story. Jake and Fred agree to meet after the meeting and look at the problem together.

- 9:10 a.m.: Maurice shares a few announcements about a group lunch on Friday and a new customer they just landed. Announcements are kept until the end of the meeting because someone will always be late and would miss them if announcements came first.

- 9:15 a.m.: Dismissed and back to work after a quick fifteen-minute meeting.

How to Get Started

If you've never had daily meetings before, you're in for a real treat! Here are a few ideas to get them rolling:

- Be sure everyone knows the format (which questions you want answered).

- Everyone must answer the questions. There are no passes, and no exceptions.

- At first, be lenient on the time restriction. *A lot* of new information is exchanged in the beginning, so you must allow communication to flow freely.

- Hold your meetings at the same time and in the same place, every day. Make daily meetings a habit, not a chore to keep track of.

- Post topics that are discussed during daily meetings on a web page or *plog*.[6]

  plog

- Pick a person to start the meeting, and then move clockwise (or counterclockwise) through the group. Randomly picking one team member after another is more apt to make them feel ambushed.

Stay Focused

Daily meetings can be a valuable tool if everyone stays on-topic. It's important to be very specific in the meeting, Don't say you're "70 percent done." Instead, say that today you added the login screen, and though it's not functional yet, it should be tomorrow. Pause for a moment if someone says, for instance, that the login screen is broken, and ask them to describe the problem in more detail (e.g., "It doesn't communicate with the authentication manager yet"). When a project is new, the tech lead runs this meeting, but eventually the leadership responsibility should rotate throughout the group. Use these daily meetings to grow your leaders in-house.

If a topic starts to take on a life of its own, or the meeting starts turning into a problem-solving session, the leader should quickly take it "offline" by having the involved team members get together privately after the main meeting. There's no reason the entire team should have to listen to Jim and Sue brainstorm for half an hour on a problem that only they have. They can give everyone a short overview of the solution after they've found it.

Several prominent development methodologies insist you limit meeting times by having everyone stand. That works, but if the meeting participants are disciplined about being brief (or if the leader is disciplined about keeping everyone on-topic) standing shouldn't be necessary. Try it both ways to see what works for your team.

---

[6]A *plog* is a project blog. A *blog* is a web log. A *web log* is an online diary, designed for easy updates. Using a plog to share information from daily meetings makes it easy to keep team members "in the know." It's a central source of information for your absent team members, other teams, or managers.

\/／ Joe Asks. . .

Our Daily Meetings Last Too Long. What Do We Do?

When you first begin to hold your daily meetings, they're going to last a while. These meetings are about sharing information, and there will be a lot of catching up to do. Your target is one or two minutes per person, but you aren't likely to achieve that brevity for several days, or even weeks. You should also expect to slow down every time you add a new team member. Daily meetings are an excellent forum to bring them up to speed!

Now, if after a couple of weeks your daily meetings are still lasting an hour, you have problems to address. You most likely have team members explaining problems and solutions in too much detail. Draw them away from the details of the fix, and try to just get the summary. For example, instead of presenting a low-level, detailed analysis of the problem, the debugging cycle, and the final solution, just say, "We had an issue with the cache not getting updating with the altered data. It is now fixed and checked in." That's all we need to know.

You can also ask team members to write down what they intend to share. It will help them organize their thoughts before the meeting, thus avoiding the "rambling report" that lasts for five minutes.

Another potential problem is having too many people in the group; we have found that daily meetings only scale to about fifteen people. In this scenario, find a way to split the daily meetings into smaller groups when possible. Put team members working in the same areas into the same meetings. Be sure to have at least one or two people overlap so that relevant information can be passed along.

You're Doing It Right If...

If you are already having daily meetings, that's great! Here are a few guidelines to be sure you stay on-track:

- Are the meetings useful? If no one in the group is learning anything, the reports might be too terse. If more details are needed in a particular area, push those topics into a side meeting with a smaller group. However, the two-minute rule is a guideline, not a law. You may find thirty seconds is just fine, or you may need three minutes.
- Are meetings consistently held the same time and place every day, or do they fluctuate? Having daily meetings at the same time and place makes it easy to remember. Meetings can move occasionally, but avoid mixing things up frequently.
- If you stopped holding the meetings, would people complain? They should! The team should come to depend on the daily meeting to stay "in the loop." If the meetings can be dismissed, then they weren't providing value. The team should rely on the daily meeting as an invaluable resource.

Warning Signs

Daily meetings are a great tool. But like any tool, they can also be harmful if handled improperly. The following are a few warning signs that your daily meetings have drifted off-course:

- Each team member takes ten minutes or more.
- One team member *consistently* takes up as much time as the rest of the team put together.
- People are heckled in a mean-spirited manner. Joking among team members is good (and to be encouraged), but if your daily meetings turn into sniping sessions, they're not productive anymore. Deal with the snipers.
- Your meetings consistently start (or finish) late.
- The meetings become content-free, with developers making claims such as "I'm still 90 percent done" or just "workin' on the Frozbot."
- Team members ramble or forget to report things they've done. Privately ask these team members to write down what they've done, so they stay focused during meetings and keep their report concise. They would also do well to have their own copy of The List to help keep them organized.

Pair Programming

Pair programming puts two team members at one computer. One types the code while the other tries to pull back and keep an eye on the big picture. One works in the details of the code and the language syntax while the other is trying to decide if a particular algorithm is the right one to use to solve a problem. The second person spots problems such as coding errors, spelling problems, and bad variable names. From time to time the developers switch roles.

Some people love the practice while others never seem to acclimate to it. We've found it to be a powerful practice when used appropriately (with the right people). For a more in-depth look at this intriguing practice, visit the aptly named web site http://www.pairprogramming.com/.

Review All Code

Small, frequent code reviews keep your code clean, simple, and tidy. You can avoid the traditionally unpleasant code reviews that involve dozens of developers and require days of preparation (a.k.a. *The Mighty Awful and Dreaded Code Review*, hereafter referred to as *MAD reviews* for your reading enjoyment). We've found code reviews can be painless when you adhere to the following rules:

- Only review a small amount of code.

- There are one or two reviewers at most.

- Review very frequently, often several times a day.

pair programming

Your goal is to move toward a habit of more frequent code reviews while not incurring the potential culture shock (or the perceived overhead) of *pair programming*. Many environments just aren't ready for that level of interaction; the cost of breath mints alone could break a thriving company! So instead, strive to review your code more often and in smaller chunks.

If a week goes by without a code review, you've allowed a lot of time for serious problems to creep into your code. You likely need an outside perspective if you have been working on a tough problem that long. It's not even that another person knows better; just the act of explaining the problem is often sufficient for you to then solve it (*The Pragmatic Programmer* calls this *rubber ducking*).[7] Waiting days before getting a code review (even if it's just an interim checkup) will probably be a long and painful experience. . . a MAD review!

To avoid MAD reviews, separate your work into the smallest possible pieces and get each one reviewed independently and committed into the source code repository. Then if there's a problem with any one area, it's easily isolated.

Programmers can easily get so caught up in the details of a particular task that they miss obvious big-picture improvements. When you stop to explain your direction and code to another person, you have to break that flow, and you'll often get a valuable fresh perspective. Sometimes we are so busy creating a road in the woods that we don't realize we are in the wrong forest, headed in the wrong direction!

Another benefit of segmenting code is that reviewers can more readily understand the code if it's divided into smaller pieces. In a fast-paced development shop, you may need to have your code reviewed many times in one day. A good rule of thumb, however, is to never work for more than two days without getting a code review. Think of code reviews like breathing. Sure, you can go a few minutes without breathing, but who wants to?

Ideally there will be one review for each feature you add (or for each bug you fix). Holding your code until you have seven new features added and fourteen bugs fixed is a recipe for the dreaded MAD review (not to mention a long, drawn-out, and unfocused effort).

If you're in the position of rewriting an intricate part of your product and you can't divide the task into smaller parts, pick one reviewer and have that person frequently do on-the-fly interim code reviews.

You'll write better code when you know someone else will see it and hold you accountable for it. This issue isn't unique to developers; it's simply human nature. Code reviews ensure that at least one other person will look at your work. You'll know that you can't take shortcuts in your code with this accountability in place.

---

[7]So called because the other person doesn't need to contribute anything to the conversation except an appropriate nod now and then. If you can't find a person, even a rubber duck will do.

Plenty of research shows the effectiveness of code reviews at detecting defects (bugs) in code. In fact, it's the number-one technique for finding bugs. There is none better. If you haven't done code reviews consistently, you may be in for a surprise at what you'll find.

We've actually seen variable names like mrHashy (Mister Hashy) for a hash table. However, after a single code review, that developer began to use more relevant variable names to avoid being teased by co-workers. Peer pressure can be painful yet effective.

Rubber ducking (explained previously) is a very effective way of finding and solving problems. By describing your code to someone, you'll suddenly realize things you forgot, recognize logic that just won't work, or find conflicts with some other area of the system. We want you to "talk" to the duck every time you check in code.

Besides the value in rubber ducking, other developers *will* spot bugs in your code. Having a fresh, second set of eyes to look over your code will often catch issues that never even occurred to you. You'll be getting a completely different point of view. Finding bugs in the development shop is always cheaper than finding them when the code is in the field. The return on this small investment is immense.

Code reviews are great for fostering knowledge sharing among team members. After collaborating on the review, your reviewer will have at least a conceptual idea of what your code does and you hope a detailed understanding of it. This has enormous mentoring benefits and helps in code maintenance as well.

Reviews provide a perfect opportunity for experienced developers to pass along code style and design techniques to less experienced programmers. Beyond the trivial technicalities (such as where the brackets go), code reviews give the veterans a chance to advise the greener developers on why one data structure might be better for this situation, or to point out that a pattern is emerging. Quite often, a reviewer will spot repeating code or functionality in these sessions, which can be moved to common base classes or utility classes. Your code becomes refactored *before* it gets checked into the source code management system.

Reviews also facilitate cross-training on small areas of coding details as well as big-picture concepts. Beyond "coding style," you are learning to "code with style."

Here are a few guidelines to assist you with code reviews.

Patterns

A *pattern* refers to the practice of documenting and naming common problems (and their solutions) that occur in real-world projects. There are several reasons to be a student of patterns. One is to give developers a common vocabulary. After developers have worked together, they develop a common set of terms that lets them communicate quickly and unambiguously. Patterns can jump-start that process and allow you to communicate clearly with someone you've just met (provided they are also familiar with the same patterns).

Another good reason to study patterns is to help you solve problems you haven't seen before. By reading and discussing various patterns, you learn how to solve many common problems. The question isn't whether you'll encounter most patterns but whether you'll recognize them when they cross your path.* Will you know how to cleanly solve the problem represented by the pattern, or will you stumble through several code iterations before you find an acceptable solution?

Design Patterns: Elements of Reusable Object-Oriented Software by Eric Gamma, Richard Helms, Ralph Johnson, and John Vlissides (a.k.a. the Gang of Four) is a great place to start.

The Humble Programmer by Edsger W. Dijkstra is a classic look at the state of computer science (including patterns) that is still very applicable today. The article was written in 1972! (See `http://www.cs.utexas.edu/users/EWD/ewd03xx/EWD340.PDF`.)

Code reviews must involve at least one other developer. In practice, it will almost always be just one other developer unless you are creating something interesting or clever that other team members want to learn about. Then feel free to include more developers. Don't go overboard, though (no more than three to four, tops); too many developers bog down the review.

Do not make code publicly available without a review. Don't add your changes to the source code from which your product is built until a review has been done. Part of the comments you include with the code's check-in should list your reviewer's name. Then, if there are questions about the reason for the code change and you're not around, there is a second person who should be able to explain it (at least at a basic level).

Refactoring

We couldn't improve on Martin Fowler's own description:

"Refactoring is a disciplined technique for restructuring an existing body of code, altering its internal structure without changing its external behavior. Its heart is a series of small behavior preserving transformations. Each transformation (called a refactoring) does little, but a sequence of transformations can produce a significant restructuring. Since each refactoring is small, it's less likely to go wrong. The system is also kept fully working after each small refactoring, reducing the chances that a system can get seriously broken during the restructuring."*

*From http://www.refactoring.com/

Never use this code review rule as an excuse to not check in your code. If your company has a source code system that holds only production code, then put your code into a private area until it's ready. This private area might be a separate code repository or another installation of the source code management system. Use whatever tools you need to get the code off your machine so that when your machine dies (as machines are prone to do), your code doesn't die with it.

Reviewers maintain the right to reject code that they find unacceptable. When you review someone's code and it isn't commented correctly, the algorithms are not efficient, or, for whatever reason, don't be afraid to ask for revisions (but don't be picky—remember there are usually many acceptable ways to achieve the same result). As a reviewer, your job is to improve the code, not to rubber-stamp it. As Eric S. Raymond says, "Many eyes make all bugs shallow."

If your code can't be explained at a level the reviewer can understand, then the code must be simplified. As a reviewer, don't sign off on anything you don't understand and feel comfortable with. After all, your name is associated with this code as the reviewer. You are, as *The Pragmatic Programmer* says, "signing your work." Be sure it's worthy of bearing your signature.

Any code changes that are made can't break any existing automated tests. (You *do* have tests, right? See Practice 7, *Use a Testing Har-*

ness, on page 43.) Don't waste your co-worker's time asking for a code review if you haven't yet run the tests. If you require existing tests to be updated, make the changes to those tests a part of the coding before the review. Any *new* tests that you are adding should be a part of the review as well. As a reviewer, always reject code changes if you think more tests are necessary.

"First, do no harm"[8] is not so much just a code review rule as it is a rule to live by in general. Code changes are never allowed to break the product. Of course, this rule is a moot point with a good test suite in place, but there's rarely an excuse to break existing functionality. Instead of breaking an existing API, add a second API that has the extra argument (or whatever) you need.

For example, if an existing function call has to be changed, establish a schedule that maps out the elimination of the existing routine. Don't just remove the routine out from under your customers (your fellow teammates or other teams within your organization); make a conscious decision whether to keep the old routine or not. The scheduled removal is also important—don't have deprecated routines that live on for years (you know who you are!).

Rotate the reviewers you use, but don't be religious about it. Occasionally having the same reviewer back to back is fine, but avoid a "buddy system" where you always review Kevin's code, and vice versa. Also, never have a single, designated (and overworked) reviewer who your entire team goes to. Both situations defeat the cross-pollination effect you're trying to encourage.

Keep code reviews informal. Rather than schedule a meeting, just drop in on a team member and ask if it's a good time for a review. Sometimes you can review the code while it's still in your editor. Sometimes you'll print out the code diffs and carry them with you. The format or venue isn't important—just get the review.

When you introduce the code review process, you may need to appoint a few senior team members to be the mandatory reviewers; one of the senior team members must participate in every review at first. You shouldn't need them to continue in this role for more than a few months. Once your team members learn the basics, the whole team will be capable of sharing the responsibility. As the proverb says, "As

---

[8]Hippocratic Oath

iron sharpens iron, so one man sharpens another."[9] The point is for the team members to work together and so improve each other. Involve your team members in the sharpening process as quickly as possible.

We worked in one shop that really illustrates how code reviews can be used to leverage your senior members. We had three very senior developers and five who were decidedly not—they weren't rank novices, but sometimes they had peculiar ideas of how to fix a problem. In order to protect the product and to bring the junior developers up to the next level, all code reviews involved one of the senior team members. This let the more experienced team members instruct and teach while catching problems before they were introduced into the product. It also made the senior team members aware of misunderstandings and real issues that the junior developers faced.

These reviews were a great help to the team. We frequently spotted repeated code and summarily pulled it out and moved it into utility classes. Reviewers caught and removed code that had nothing to do with assigned work (otherwise known as *freelance refactoring*) and rejected uncommented code outright. As the team moved forward, an imperceptible (but very important) change took place.

Each of the junior team members started picking up good habits, one code review at a time. They started cleaning up code before the reviews, adding meaningful variable names, comments, and such before they were asked. Long, cumbersome routines became short and manageable.

Even better, the lessons taught in the code reviews stuck. After about three months, we changed the code review policy so that any team member could do the reviews.

If one or two of your developers routinely miss things in reviews, you should double-check their work using the code change notifications (see Practice 14, *Send Code Change Notifications*, on page 98). Monitoring the code change notifications gives you an easy, noninvasive way to keep an eye on any member of the shop without sitting in their office and looking over their shoulder.

At times you will be engrossed in a problem and would be completely derailed by stopping to participate in a code review. Trying to get your head back into the problem would cost you a great deal of time.

---

[9]Proverbs 27:17, NIV

Virtual Code Reviews

Over time, you will learn what types of things specific reviewers will look for. For instance, Jared once wrote an intricate piece of code and had it working to his satisfaction. He then did a "virtual review," trying to spot what two of his most senior co-workers would target. After implementing the changes he thought each of them would have suggested, he had them actually review the code. They loved it! The three of them had reviewed so much code together that he was able to analyze code from their point of view. Jared had learned what two developers (with many more years experience than him) valued and was able to use that experience to improve his own work. That's why you do code reviews; you're not only building good product but also building good developers.

(Remember the discussion on interruptions? See Practice 11, *A Tech Leads*, on page 69.) If someone comes in asking for a code review (or for anything for that matter) when you're immersed in a problem, tell them you are "deep" right now and have them come back later. On the other hand, if you're the one looking for a reviewer and someone says they're deep, either go away and wait for them to get to a good stopping point or find someone else.

Much of the work related to software development is mental—getting our heads wrapped around a problem and staying there until we get it solved. It's not an insult to ask someone to come back later when you're in a situation that requires concentration. In some shops this concept comes naturally, but in others it seems to be completely foreign. It should always be okay to ask someone to come back in thirty minutes or after lunch.

> **TIP 17**
>
> It's okay to say "later"

Your management must *require* code reviews. If there's no management buy-in, no one in your shop has any official motivation to participate. In other words, if no one has been told to help you, they probably won't make time to do it, especially when deadlines are tight.

If your shop doesn't have a mandatory code review policy, you can still ask your teammates for code reviews. The entire team won't get the benefit, but your own code will improve. The people who review your code will also learn the benefits of code reviews over time.

Don't wait too long for any one person to have the time to do a review; walk around the shop, and find somebody who's not deep into a problem. Walk to the other side of the building if you have to, but find someone. If it's someone you haven't used for a code review before, this is a great opportunity for them to see what you do.

These quick code reviews promote mentoring without the overhead of a formal program. By varying the developers you work with for code reviews, you get the benefit of a variety of developers' experience and expertise. Each reviewer will point out different ways to solve the same problem. Some better, some not, but all different.

> TIP 18
>
> Always review all code

The goal is to learn how to think creatively while also improving your product. Learn to look at your own problems from different points of view. These short code reviews will become second nature over time, and just like microwave ovens, you'll wonder how you ever survived without them. Practical discussions of algorithm analysis or resource constraints are lessons that are taught (and remembered) because you have a practical and immediate application.

Rather than academic book learning or certifications, you'll be sitting at the workbench of various craftsmen (some masters, some apprentices) learning a little bit from each one, adding their tricks to your own, until one day you are one of the master craftsmen yourself.

How to Get Started

Code reviews are great tools! Once you get in the habit, you'll wonder how you ever wrote decent code without them. Use these tips to get started:

- Be sure everyone understands the type of code review you have planned. Review frequently on smaller blocks of code. Don't wait for weeks, accumulating hundreds or thousands of lines of changes. No MAD reviews for your team!

- Have one of your senior team members sit in on each code review for the first few weeks or months. This is a great way to share knowledge and get the reviews on a solid foundation.

- Make sure your code reviews are lightweight. It's better to review too little code than too much. Having two overlapping reviews is better than having one larger one.

- Introduce a code change notification system (see Practice 14, *Send Code Change Notifications*, on the following page) at this time. It's a great complement to your code reviews, and it helps to remind team members who forget to ask for reviews.

- Make sure you have management buy-in before requiring all team members to participate.

You're Doing It Right If...

- Do code reviews get an automatic approval? This shouldn't happen unless everyone on the team is perfect.
- Does every code review have major rewrites? If so, it indicates a problem somewhere: either with the coder, with the reviewer, or with the tech lead (who gave the directions that the coder and reviewer are using).
- Do code reviews happen frequently? If the time between reviews is measured in weeks, you're waiting too long.
- Are you rotating reviewers?
- Are you learning from the code reviews? If not, start asking more questions during your code reviews.

Warning Signs

- Code reviews are infrequent.
- The majority of code reviews are painful.
- People avoid checking in their code because they don't want a code review.
- Team members who have reviewed code can't explain what it does or why it was written.
- Junior team members review only other junior member's code.
- Similarly, senior team members review only other senior member's code.
- A single team member is everyone's preferred reviewer.

> ### Information Radiators
>
> According to Alistair Cockburn:
>
> "An information radiator displays information in a place where passersby can see it. With information radiators, the passersby don't need to ask questions; the information simply hits them as they pass.
>
> "Two characteristics are key to a good information radiator. The first is that the information changes over time. This makes it worth a person's while to look at the display. The other characteristic is that it takes very little energy to view the display."
>
> From (Coc01).

▶ 14 Send Code Change Notifications

When you edit code, an automatic build system can notice the change and rebuild the project (see Practice 4, *Build Automatically*, on page 31). Your next step is to publish that information so that every member of the team knows what changed.

A change notification system pushes this information out to your entire shop, not just your immediate co-workers. The effect from this type of knowledge sharing can be quite amazing.

Similar to Alistair Cockburn's "information radiators," you are making information available. Your team can use it or ignore it, but the information is being put out there for you. In fact, this practice doesn't make you fetch the data; it pushes it to your desktop.

Each time we've introduced this practice, a sizable percentage of the shop has been opposed to the practice before they've tried it.

After about a month, the worst complainers always come by to apologize and tell us how useful the tool has become to them. This technique consistently brings the most resistance, but after a short time everyone becomes acclimated to having the notifications available. It quickly becomes a vital resource.

A typical code change notification might look something like this:

```
In the DB package, added createRecord() to TdDataFile

Index: com/tde/db/TdDataFile.java
=====================================================================
RCS file: c:\apps\cvs\cvsroot\WeissDB\com\tde\db\TdDataFile.java,v
retrieving revision 1.3
diff -r1.3 TdDataFile.java
381a382,401
>   /**
>    * Returns a new instance of the record type stored in this table.
>    * @return TdRecord - The new instance of the record.
>    * @exception ClassNotFoundException - This exception is thrown if the
>    * class name stored can not be found.
>    * @exception InstantiationException - This exception is thrown if the
>    * class name stored can not be created.
>    * @exception IllegalAccessException - This exception is thrown if the
>    * class representing the class name stored has the wrong scope or there
>    * is no 0 parameter ctor.
>    */
>   public TdRecord createRecord() throws ClassNotFoundException,
>             InstantiationException,
>             IllegalAccessException {
>       // Create a new instance of the record
>       return (TdRecord) (Class.forName(getRecordName()).newInstance());
>   }
>
>
```

There are two ways you can implement this type of system. The preferred way is to have your changes automatically emailed to each team member. Most automatic build systems will send changes for you (and they'll usually publish your changes to a web page and RSS feeds as well). The other way to implement this system is manually. Each team member would need to isolate the differences in their code and the old version of the files and to email the differences to everyone in the group. (We call this process *mailing the diffs*.)

However you implement it, change notifications should go out to your team each time code is checked into the source code management system. Your notification emails must include the following:

- Reviewer's name.
- Purpose of the code change or addition (for instance, which bug you've fixed or which feature you've added).
- Difference between the new code and old code (Any major source code management system will generate this report for you.) If you've completely rewritten a block of code so large that it would make a diff meaningless, just include the new code. The same applies to new files.

Unexpected Benefits

Several years ago, we were refactoring a rather complicated and long-running algorithm, trying to make it run faster. When finished, we sent the customary code change notification to the team. An hour or so later, a member of the team dropped in with a major rewrite of the entire algorithm. His changes ran an order of magnitude faster.

This team member had a doctorate's degree in a field that involved advanced algorithm analysis. Everyone knew his background, but it had been a hectic several months, and it never crossed anyone's mind to have him review the changes. However, when he saw the email and read the comment block, it caught his attention. With his background, he immediately spotted an "obvious" improvement to the entire algorithm that no one else had thought of. This story is a classic example of the unexpected benefits you receive from code notifications. They can (and often do) yield surprising benefits.

Keep Everyone Informed

Code notifications are an easy way to foster accountability among your team members. They'll help catch the maverick developer who isn't getting code reviews or who adds code that isn't directly called for by a bug or feature on The List.

You will notice who the most active writers and reviewers are pretty quickly. When someone doesn't commit code for a week, your tech lead can go visit and make sure they're not stuck or off-track. At one company, by request, we added the CEO to the code notification list so that he could keep a close eye on the "pulse of the project." Visibility to management is difficult on most software projects, and this is an easy way to help push information out.

Ignore Them If You Like

You may choose not to use the notification emails as any type of reference. Eventually, though, you'll probably find yourself peeking at them from time to time to get some bit of information. Before you know it, you'll find you've come to depend on them and use them every day.

When our editor, Andy Hunt, was reviewing this manuscript, he marked this section to be questioned. *(That's publishing-speak for "Delete it!"— Ed.)* Coincidentally (and before we'd had time to talk with him about the section's worth), he saw this technique being used very successfully

Sign Your Work

The Pragmatic Programmer reminds us to always work in such a way that we're proud of what we've done. Whether your work is crafting software solutions or building cathedrals, you should work as if everything you touch will be examined by your co-workers and customers under a very bright light. If you knew that the wood panel you were making would be the front door of the cathedral instead of the back of a closet, would you work on it differently?

Signing your work does *not* mean that you have exclusive ownership rights or that no one else can edit the code. It means that you worked on the code and will stand behind your work. If someone needs to ask questions about the code, your name is first on the list and the teammates who reviewed your code will be second. If someone finds a problem with your code, they'll knew who touched the code and who can fix any problems.

Becoming skilled at your craft includes becoming an expert at specific sections of your code base—and there is nothing wrong with that. Doctors specialize, as do most professions. You might visit your family doctor for an annual physical, but when problems are found, we always move to an expert quickly. Expecting every developer on the team to learn every section of code is not realistic on a real-world project. By signing your work you are announcing that this is a piece of the code base that you know and can work on. Forcing developers to play "musical chairs" doesn't ensure that everyone becomes an expert on all the code. It ensures that no one becomes an expert on *any* of it. While there may be cases where keeping everyone down to the same level may be beneficial, we prefer to have specialists around, for both code and medicine.

while visiting a client. After seeing it in use with its practical benefits, he let us keep it in the book. After all, if it works, it's pragmatic.

How to Get Started

There are several ways you can introduce code change notifications. We've used both manual and automatic systems. With a manual system, you type emails by hand (pasting in code diffs by hand) and send them to team members. With an automatic system, a program that watches your SCM generates notices and sends emails.

Both are valid approaches, but automatic is always preferable. However, getting an automatic system in place may be difficult in your environment; if that's the case, use the manual method.

Make sure your team knows about the notifications before they start arriving.

You're Doing It Right If...

Notifications must be regular and trustworthy.

Don't send out five-meg diffs!

Warning Signs

The only real problem you need to watch for here is dependability. The notifications must be reliable. If your team members don't believe the mail will be sent after code changes, they won't come to depend on notifications. This is easier to fix with an automatic system than with a manual one, but in either case, you must take this problem into account.

15 ▶ Putting It All Together

Unlike more complicated, full-featured methodologies, you really can *do* this. You can start today and see at least some benefits right away. You'll see more benefits over time, of course, and the more you invest in your methods of work, the more benefits you'll see. There are no silver bullets, but the techniques we've presented here help prevent a large number of common disasters while staying out of your way as much as possible. Implementing these techniques will make you look like a programming god, but really you're just leveraging the experience of others. You'll "stand on the shoulders of giants," as the saying goes.

The following is a summary of the techniques we've discussed in this chapter. Copy this, put it on your wall, and *follow it*. You'll soon wonder how you ever did without it.

- The List:
    - Publicly available
    - Prioritized
    - On an estimated time line
    - Living
- Tech lead:
    - Manages projects' feature lists
    - Tracks developers' current tasks and status
    - Helps assign priorities to each feature
    - Insulates the team from external distractions
- Daily meetings:
    - Keep them short
    - Require specifics
    - List problems, but don't solve them
- Code reviews:
    - Small amount of code reviewed
    - One or two reviewers
    - Happen frequently
    - Don't publish code without a review
- Code change notifications:
    - Email and publish notifications
    - List the reviewer's name
    - List purpose of the code change or addition
    - Include the diff or file itself, size permitting

Chapter 4

Tracer Bullet Development

When you fire a machine gun at night, it's difficult to see where your bullets are going. Even when the target is in plain sight, hitting a target in the dark is not a trivial task. Fortunately for machine-gun owners, someone invented *tracer bullets*. Every so often, a tracer bullet is mixed in with the regular bullets. Tracer bullets contain a small amount of flare-like material that burns when fired, leaving a long, arcing trace in the sky.

tracer bullets

So what do tracer bullets have to do with your software development work?

When you fire a tracer bullet, you can see exactly where it's going. This lets you adjust your aim—in real time, under real conditions—to get the bullets right on target.

Tracer Bullet Development

The practice of Tracer Bullet Development (TBD) does the same thing for your software project: it lets you see where things are headed as soon as you start and helps you aim continuously long before you're done. TBD is the most effective way we've found to develop software—it's very easy to use and extremely powerful. In fact, it's so important that we'll take this entire chapter to look at this one practice.

A development process (be it TBD or another process, like RUP or XP[1]) is the string that ties all the facets of your work together. It unites a hodgepodge of practices, tools, and techniques into a cohesive whole.

---

[1]For more details on different methodologies, see Appendix F on page 181.

Your process is a set of steps you link together to build products in a repeatable manner. It enables you to build products time after time in the same way, using the same tools and taking your development effort from a hit-or-miss gamble to being repeatable and dependable. When your sales and marketing team present you with a product idea, your team will be able to deliver the product every time. Perhaps the delivery won't be on the sales department's ideal time line, but the company will be able to count on you to deliver what you promise in the time frame in which you promise it.

Popular Process Problems

There are many popular processes available to you today, but most can be both overwhelming and frustrating.

One category of processes will offer you a virtual banquet, where you have to choose from hundreds of practices and assign dozens of roles. Unfortunately, the various options tend to be so complicated that you're forced to hire specialized consultants just to know which practices to even evaluate. Implementation and usage of these practices are equally difficult—most practitioners spend as much time administering these systems as they do writing code.

Another major category pretends to be flexible, telling you to "roll your own" process, but then insists that you use their core (and frankly, sometimes strange) practices. You are allowed to use any practice you like, as long as it's the practices they suggest. Devotees of these processes try to impose their alien culture on your shop. Imposing culture usually fails, and followers of this category then blame you instead. They know it's the "right way" to work, so the fault must lie with you.

In either case, introducing these types of new practices generally throws the entire shop into such shock that management runs away from any other new process attempts, ever again.

At the end of the day, the people who matter (your customers and end users) don't care which process you use. They only want to know whether you've delivered a solid product and if you can do it again.

There are only two real questions your process must answer to:

- Does it work for you?

- Is it sustainable?

Defining Your Process

Without exception, every shop we've encountered that didn't have a well-defined process was unable to deliver an on-time product with the expected feature set. This has as much to do with the absence of a process as it does the lack of thought that goes on in such shops. Don't let this happen to you: take the time to understand what you're doing and why.

On a practical note, any process that prohibits any other best practices from being introduced is almost certainly a bad process. *Beware any process or methodology that claims to be the exclusive solution to every problem for all projects.* This magic cure-all is just modern snake oil. Embrace a methodology that encourages periodic reevaluation and inclusion of whatever practices work well on your project. Be sure your process is a flexible one—don't be afraid to change or adjust your process to see if a new, better practice can fit in. If you have a new idea, drop it in for a few weeks. If it works out, great! Make it a permanent addition. Otherwise, revise it or get rid of it. This experimentation is how you'll find out what fits your shop the best. There are no sacred cows in a good process. Anything that works well can stay; anything that isn't working must be removed or revised.

Because every project is different, and every team is unique, *you* are the only one qualified to judge what works and what doesn't.

For example, take the idea of a four-week iteration (or sprint). Using this practice, a shop plans to have a new set of deliverables every four weeks. We've seen management that religiously adheres to this standard even though the developers and testers constantly protest that it's not enough time in their particular environment. This shop should consider trying five-week iterations, or perhaps three-week iterations. And who says iterations have to be back to back? If it feels rushed, take a break between iterations to test, fix bugs, or brainstorm for the next round.

The goal isn't to have four-week iterations; it's to turn out great software. If a well-known practice isn't working in your shop, tinker with it. There's not much out there that can't stand a little improvement. Being agile means you must adapt whatever isn't working to better suit your particular needs.

> **Canned Data**
>
> You might often find yourself in a situation where you need reproducible input or output data, especially for testing and Tracer Bullet Development. We call predefined data *canned data*. Canned data is often used for tests because it provides a reproducible input for the tests. Using it with Tracer Bullet Development allows your components to return "valid" data, appearing to work long before the components are fully functional.

> **TIP 19**
>
> The goal is software, not compliance

With these caveats in mind, we'll take a closer look at Tracer Bullet Development. You can use it as a starting point for your shop or use it just as is. The important thing is knowing what a process *is* and having a well-thought-out process in place. Keep it light enough to avoid "analysis paralysis" or "infrastructure overload" but detailed enough to keep work on-track. TBD does a good job of striking that balance.

How Does It Work?

TBD doesn't try to change the way you work; it wraps around the way you're already working. It's intended to be noninvasive, existing seamlessly with your other practices. It's also one of the smallest processes available and is very easy to use.

canned data

You create an end-to-end working system when you use TBD, but the system components are all hollow objects. You write code for all the big pieces of your system, but the objects aren't doing any work; for example, your login routine might accept only a single user name ("Fred") and generate a valid login. Your database access layer returns data, but it's really returning *canned data*, not data from a database. Coincidentally, in the early stages of a project, the interior of each object needs to be finished; it's waiting "to be done," so the TBD acronym is quite appropriate.

Here's how to put Tracer Bullet Development to work:

> ## Mock Objects
>
> This is the practice of using dummy objects to replace objects in your system that aren't practical to test against. For instance, if you work at a large telecommunications company, you may not have complete access to a five-million-dollar switch. Rather than wait for your turn at the switch to test your code, use a mock object that acts like the switch and use that. This is often done for large databases, expensive hardware, etc. For more information, see `http://www.mockobjects.com`.

Identify the major parts of your project, and divide your product into blocks of related functionality. For example, you might have blocks called *client*, *web server*, and *database layer*.

Define the information that the blocks need to exchange and document the information with method signatures. These areas of layer interactions are called *interfaces*. Don't worry about getting this perfect the first few times. *interfaces*

Give each block to a different developer, team of developers, or corner of your mind (if you're working solo).

Write just enough code to make everything look as if it works. Think of it as an entire application of *Mock Objects*. Each layer appears to be authenticating users or fetching data (or whatever your application needs to do), but in reality, each layer is stubbed out and is simply returning canned data. *Mock Objects*

With this thin, skeletal framework in place, you can begin to fill in the real logic inside each block.

Finally, and most importantly remember that interfaces will change and evolve throughout the project. Your first shot will always miss the target, so be flexible and adjust your aim at any point. When another team approaches you for new interfaces, or to make changes to existing ones, go ahead and make the change. This is *soft*ware, after all.

Define Your System Objects

Your first step is to identify the layers into which your application can be divided. Good examples of these objects are *client*, *server*, and

Interfaces

When we use the word *interfaces*, we're not talking about C++, C#, or Java interfaces. We're talking about the routines that program layers use to pass information. An interface is an API between program areas. It's the point at which the two different areas interact, or *interface*.

---

database. You want to be careful not to define lower-level objects. Of course, your definition of *lower level* will vary wildly in a client-server application as opposed to an API-based database library.

system object

Be sure that each *system object* you define can stand alone. If you can create an object with clean lines of separation from other parts of the system, then it can be a system object. We'll look at an example in a moment.

By keeping these objects as large as you can, your teams will be able to work independently for longer stretches of time. Defining every single object in the system at this point wastes a great deal of your time; creating and maintaining the interfaces for that many low-level objects (objects such as `Person` or `Address`) is overkill at this stage.

A system object must be large enough to justify a person or team working alone for some length of time. You also must be able to create a clean line between each system object. A logging manager is a good example of a system object. A logging manager can have a well-defined API, can be reused by many other system objects, and can be rewritten behind the scenes without any of your consumers being aware of the change.

A database manager is another good example. When you define an API for your data access, you'll encapsulate the rest of your system objects from details about how data is stored and retrieved. A database manager is also a place where you'll likely do some type of rewrite. Perhaps you'll switch databases or just tweak for performance, but without a clean API, you'll have to retool other system objects as well.

As an example, let's say your project is an application that asks a server to fetch data, analyze it, and then return the results. For this scenario, you have four major system objects:

> ### ⅓ Joe Asks...
>
> #### Can Tracer Bullets Handle a Complicated System?
>
> In our example we show a very simple architecture with one system object at each level (sometimes known as a *totem pole* architecture). Rest assured that our example has one object at distinct levels for simplicity, not because TBD requires it.

- Client layer
- Web server layer
- Data cruncher layer
- Database access layer

By setting up very large objects at this stage, you decouple the major parts of your project. For example, our sample application has a web server layer, a data cruncher layer and a database access layer. These three objects are often lumped together in a single object called *the server*. With a single server object, all the functionality that we separated into the three layers is intermingled behind a single set of server interfaces. When you use a decoupled architecture, it's trivial for different teams to work in parallel on different layers. It's also easier to automate test suites that validate your layer's functionality.

Think of your server objects as pots and your development teams as cooks. Sure, if the pot is big enough, everyone can stir in the same pot. It's a lot easier if everyone has their own pot.

A different development team works on each layer, and each team assumes that their layer exists on a different computer. This means that all communication between layers is over the network. This gets you several big benefits.

First, no one can circumvent the documented interfaces and access your code directly. (This tends to happen more often the night before big deadlines!) Running layers on other machines provides a hard demarcation that can't be circumvented.

The second benefit to this architecture is scalability. When one of your layers requires more resources, you can move it to a larger machine.

It's impossible to achieve this type of scalability in a traditional tightly coupled architecture without a major rewrite. Several (if not all) of the layers will probably end up on the same machine, but it's no longer a requirement. When any layer starts to impact performance, you can simply move it to another machine (more on that a bit later).

If it pains you to gloss over this much detail and use such large objects, don't worry. You can create fine-grained objects when you start adding functionality to the system objects. If you tried to define every object in the system this early, you would invest a lot of the entire team's time before you prove the design as a whole works. At best, you will waste the time of team members who don't need to understand the objects you use to represent an address. At worst, you will waste the entire team's time learning about objects that you will throw away later. Keep low-level code TBD (To Be Done) as long as possible.

Collaborate to Define Interfaces

Next, the teams working on adjacent layers meet, and together they flesh out the interfaces that their layers share. If you know that the client application needs to log in, then you know that a log in call must exist in the web server layer. The teams collaborate and come to an agreement on the method names and signatures. You then code each method but return only canned data. For example, a dummy login routine always succeeds if your name is Fred and fails for any other user.

In these meetings, you begin to define how the layers will communicate with each other. Will you write a native application using CORBA, an HTML client talking to a servlet, or a C# application talking to an ASP server? Will the web server use CGI with Perl or use HTML with Ruby? Your teams flesh out such details among themselves so that after this meeting (or as many meetings as it takes), everyone involved knows and understands the interface points between each layer.

As you can see, you accomplish a great deal more than simply documenting method signatures in these meetings. In the process of defining layers, server types, and communication details, you also define your architecture.

The best architectures aren't defined by an "architect" in an ivory tower; they are collaborative efforts. Instead of having a guru drive by and drop a completed architecture document in your lap, your team works

Design Tricks

The following are a few tricks you can use to make your interface design meetings go smoothly:

- Always have a single person lead your meetings. This person always has the floor and must "give permission" before anyone can speak. Having a single person lead the meeting will help prevent the meeting from turning into a shouting match.

- Record notes on a white board throughout the meeting. With the information on a white board, everyone can see what method signatures you've agreed on in real time. If you take notes on paper, inevitably someone won't see what you've written.

- Andy Hunt suggests trying using LEGOs or wooden building blocks for the objects in your system. You help the more junior members understand the system and the relationships between the different objects when you give them something tangible to see and touch. Sometimes the intangible nature of our work makes the system components difficult to visualize and understand. Whether you draw objects on the white board or move blocks on the table, have a visual or tactile representation of your system.

- Record the interfaces and publish them. You can use a printed document, a web page, or a wiki, but regardless of what medium you use, you must make the information publicly available. The last place you want to keep secrets is an object's interface.

- Hold your meetings where you won't be interrupted. You want to minimize the number of times you have to shift gears and answer questions.

together, leveraging and increasing everyone's experience. While there are great benefits to including an architect in the process to help lead the discussion, products designed in a vacuum by an architect with no recent product experience are a disaster waiting to happen.

There are many benefits to this style of group architecture design:

- Defining the product becomes a learning process for your team members, especially junior ones.

- When your team creates the architecture together, they gain an overall understanding of the *entire* system.

- Your team feels a great deal of ownership of the system that they designed. You never get that same feeling when you're assigned a specification created by some cloistered, monk-like architect.

The goal is to avoid the disenfranchisement so many developers feel when they are told to code, not think. When your architecture is imposed on your team and the legitimate concerns of frustrated developers are ignored, developers feel like cogs in a machine. The coders "in the trenches" who intimately understand the technology have no way to improve the overall system, and that experience can be incredibly frustrating. By including everyone, you build a better system and train your team members at the same time.

> **TIP 20**
>
> Architect as a group

Write the Interface Stubs

This is the easiest part of the project. Remember to keep everything as simple as possible. The goal of an interface is to be just thin enough to compile and be used.

If your server requires a `Login` interface, your code should contain nothing other than the correct arguments and some indication of success (such as a return code). For instance, your login call might look like this:

```
Boolean Login (String userName, String password) {
    return True;
}
```

Raise Your Bus Number

Your *bus number* is the number of developers you'd have to lose to disable your project. Whether they quit or get hit by the proverbial bus, losing this many people will derail your project.

If you have a single superstar who keeps all the project details to themselves, you have a bus number of *one*, and that's a problem. If every member of your team can fill in for any other person, then you would have to lose your entire team for the project to be completely derailed. Ideally, you want your bus number to be equal to the number of your team members, but at the very least you should work to raise the number. If the loss of one or two key people can devastate your product, take steps to raise that number.

Tracer Bullet Development automatically raises your bus number. When team members from adjacent layers work together to define their shared interfaces, they are sharing knowledge about each layer's operations. This picture, shared between the two teams, makes it possible for your group's members to move between layers more easily. At a minimum, everyone has a basic understanding of what adjacent layers do and how they work.

If you've never considered your project's bus number, take a few minutes to survey your team. What's your bus number? What steps can you take to raise it?

Note that the code examples in this section are pseudo-code, not a specific language. We use pseudo-code when we design to avoid "holy wars" regarding language syntax. At this point we're focusing on the interface, not the implementation.

You might add the routine `AnalyzeDataSet`, which accepts a data set (which it ignores) and then returns a small "analyzed" data set. Of course, both data sets are canned data. It might look like this:

```
DataSet AnalyzeDataSet (DataSet thisDataSet) {
    DataSet thatDataSet = new DataSet();

    thatDataSet.add(2);
    thatDataSet.add(3);
    thatDataSet.add(5);

    return thatDataSet;
}
```

You don't care whether the user is logged in or the "analyzed" data set is correct. What you have is a routine that a client can invoke and use, and that's the goal at this stage.

Be sure to finish one pass at all your interfaces before you insert code that adds functionality. Resist the temptation to start coding something easy. Once you've added a small bit of functionality, it gets harder to resist adding another and another. The next thing you know, your teammates on the adjacent layers can't compile their code because your interfaces haven't been finished yet.

If you have an area where you feel strongly about adding a note so you won't forget an idea, add comments instead. Perhaps even document what you think will be the major parts of the routine or warnings about a potential problem. This will enable you to persist the information without delving into real code.

Once you've completed this step, your interfaces (or APIs) are established, and each team has a clear understanding of their role in the project. Each side now knows what areas they have to work on, and they also have a skeleton to start filling in.

Make Your Layers Talk

Now that you have completed your stubs, you're ready to start making them talk to the other layers in your system.

That may not sound important, but you'll be surprised how many seemingly insignificant details will not work together the way everyone thought they would. Once you start adding callbacks, using different CORBA vendors, and trying to use Java RMI on different network subnets through firewalls and the like, it's a whole different ballgame from "Hello, World!"

If you catch these incompatibilities early, you can change your architecture before your team writes 10,000 lines of code around these assumptions. Coincidentally, you avoid looking bad in front of your boss when, after six months of development, the entire system won't quite work the way you told him it would.

Your client code can now access the server and ask it to validate your login credentials. Given the stub we showed previously, you know that the login request will always succeed. At this point you're verifying that your client can talk to the server and that the server can relay the success or failure of the login attempt.

Just as the client is now talking to the server, the server will need to access its adjacent layers as well. Inside the login call, your code can now ask the database access layer for the information related to the user logging in.

```
Boolean Login(String userName, String password) {
    String realPassword = getPassword(userName);
    Boolean login =  False;
    if(realPassword.equals(password)) {
        login = True;
    }
    return login;
}
```

Of course, the database access layer isn't actually looking up anyone's information. It's returning canned data (asdf for instance) for every password request (and this would be documented in the interface design meeting notes).

With this addition, we now have the client talking to the web server, which then talks to the database access layer. In other words, you have a tracer bullet that fires from the client, goes through your major layers, and then goes back again. You've just proven that your entire system can "talk!" As every team puts code into their stubs to access the other layers, they are proving that every technology involved actually can interoperate. You've reached a milestone that many major projects reach only after writing thousands of lines of unintentionally useless code.

But don't get too confident until you've put your system into a live production environment. Will the customer run part of the system behind a firewall? Then you should too!

We're not saying that every workstation in the building should be a mirror of your production environment. However, at least one workstation should, and your automated build and test machine would be an ideal candidate. If that isn't available, having at least one developer working in that environment every day will catch errors quickly.

Tip 21

If production uses it, you should too

Be sure that your system runs before you start adding functionality. Adding functionality will take many more development hours than building this hollow shell. Be sure that your hollow shell works end to end before you invest time to make it do the real work.

Your project now has the following:

- A complete, documented, architecture.

- A proof of concept that shows your architecture works. You can make a client invocation and see it run, end-to-end.

- Clear boundaries between teams.

- Clear demarcations between areas of product functionality.

- Experience meeting with the teams responsible for adjacent code layers. Having all your teams talking with each other is a huge benefit.

Fill In the Stubs with Functional Code

You now have an end-to-end working system. Every piece can talk to each other, and all the code compiles and runs. It's time for you to start making it do real work.

Even as good fences make good neighbors, good interfaces make for good team interactions. Each team can now work in complete isolation if necessary and can start to fill in the logic behind each interface. Each of your teams now has a basic framework that they can begin to fill out. You can do whatever you like, as long as you don't break the existing interfaces. No one can change APIs between layers unless both teams agree.

The temptation you will have at this point is to start adding simple functionality, like making Login work properly. Resist that urge! Up until the point the product actually ships, having a working Login is a luxury. You don't need it for customer demos, and it doesn't prevent you from doing other development work. However, having your core functionality working is not a luxury. If the core functionality doesn't work, you don't have a product.

As you start to implement functionality, target any area that contains new technology, is inherently difficult, or is core to your product. If your project is using a third-party graphing package that no one has used before, you should integrate that first. If you have data analysis routines that are the core of your product, write them and get them working first. In other words, solve the hard problems early. Leave the easy stuff until later.

> **TIP 22**
>
> ## Solve the hardest problems first

If you're going to have problems that take extra time or if you need to replace components, catch the issues early. Don't wait until the last week to discover that you can't really handle a million data points or that your widgets don't work quite the way you hoped they would. Figure this out early, and get the problem fixed or the time line adjusted. If you're using The List (see Practice 10, *Work from The List*, on page 57), you'll remove a few lower-priority items to cover the lost time. However, you'll have no room to reschedule if you leave your most difficult problems until the end.

Taking care of nasty problems early removes risks from your project time lines early. This has the nice side effect of making sure that the end of your project is the *easy* work. While most teams are scrambling to get the hard parts working, your team will be finishing up `Login`.

This stage is also a good place to spot potential performance problems, especially related to network traffic. As you start filling in code, keep an eye on functions that take a long time. Functionality like locating CORBA objects on the network fall into this category. If you use these routines sparingly, they will cause no problems. However, you'll find your project's performance slowing to a crawl if you invoke them frequently. If a piece of code is slow in your development environment, it won't have a chance on a customer's heavily used server.

Refactor and Refine

Being a real-world project, the interfaces between layers will naturally change and evolve as the project continues to be clarified and better understood. These ongoing improvements are to be expected; the code's evolution is perfectly normal.[2] Your change process won't be painful,

---

[2]Jim Highsmith observes that it's important to get it right the *last* time, not the first time.

Broken Windows

No one is allowed to break your system once it's running.

The original "stubbed out" system continues to run throughout the life of the project. Your functionality expands as you write code for specific interfaces, but the other interfaces should continue to run. Treat any break in your product as a broken window (described in (HT00)). Once a single function is broken, it's easy to break a second, third, or fourth. However, no one wants to be the person who first breaks a working system. Because your tracer bullet system is up and running very early in the time line, your product stays clean every day and creeping problems don't accumulate.

though: your teams have worked together already, and you probably have developed a great rapport.

Waterfall development model

Many processes block off your project into phases, much like the old *Waterfall development model*. Waterfall development has a very strict set of phases, one after another: requirements, specifications, design, implementation, testing, and maintenance. Of course, using phases like this assumes that you have a perfect understanding of the problem before you start and that you can accurately schedule each phase. It's ridiculous to think your team will thoroughly understand the details of any large software project before it starts. In our experience, phased projects generally fail to meet deadlines and deliver a product.

Instead, you need to stay flexible throughout the entire software development cycle instead of trying to force your project's time line into predefined phases. As your teams add real functionality to their stub code, they will discover that one interface needs an extra variable passed in or that another interface was missed entirely. You can add this functionality at any time. The point of your process is to allow you to make these incremental changes as you need them, rather than when the schedule permits them.

When you make these changes, publicize them so that other teams that use the same interfaces won't be surprised. If need be, just add a new interface with the extra variable instead of pulling one out from under another team. Remember that you never break the builds in a tracer bullet project. Any code that you add should extend the system, not break it.

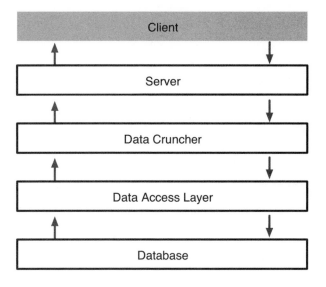

Figure 4.1: A SYSTEM WITH FOUR MAJOR LAYERS

You will also realize at some point that code you've written needs to be thrown out. Maybe the code is too slow or it returns the wrong results. Any one of a thousand things may be wrong with it. Feel free to completely refactor or rewrite code, as long as the interface still works the same way. You can make these changes at any time in a Tracer Bullet Development project. The rule is that you can't change the interface that the other teams use without consent, but you can change the code behind those routines at will. As long as the interface works the same way, the other teams won't be aware that you've changed the code. Their code should still use your interface the same way, only now it runs faster or returns the correct data.

A Brief Example

We once worked on a project that illustrates the huge architectural advantages of this type of layered encapsulation. It was a project with four system objects: a client layer, a web server layer, a data cruncher layer, and a database access layer (see Figure 4.1).

The project was for a biotech firm. The client application allowed the user to upload a set of grouped data points (one module took drug

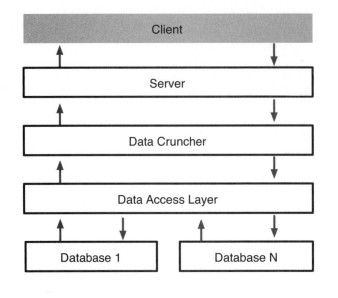

Figure 4.2: A FOUR-LAYER SYSTEM WITH MULTIPLE DATABASES

molecules, another DNA segments, and so on), and the system would look for things the data points had in common. The database contained experiment results, information mined from scholarly publications, various public biological databases, and other sources. The database was rather complicated to say the least. Given the way the data was connected, finding relationships among the uploaded data involved large amounts of database accesses and number crunching.

If you uploaded ten DNA snippets, the system would look for connections between each snippet. How many were mentioned in the same scientific articles? How many were in the same DNA strands in a mouse or a human? Were any of the larger strands mentioned in articles? Were there other experiments involving these strands? Were there known relationships between the various data points that were published in any form? The number of data points to be examined increased by an order of magnitude after relationships were followed through a few steps. Then various statistical analysis routines were run to find relationships or to graph the results.

The system was very straightforward. The client application uploads requests. After the user uploaded the information to the web server, it would group the data and send the groups to data crunchers. Data crunchers would ask the data layer for the information about each data point and then begin analyzing the results. The web server would collate all the results and send it back to the client.

While adding features to this project, we noticed that our database layer had become a bottleneck. The queries were simply running too slowly. We optimized the database calls but did not change the API that the data cruncher layer used. The alterations were transparent to the data cruncher layer. The data cruncher layer asked for data the same way, but the data access layer returned the data more quickly.

However, as the project requirements continued to change, we needed to support a much higher level of data throughput than we had originally envisioned. We adopted a very radical approach; we distributed the underlying database calls across a farm of database servers. We ran client queries in parallel on different machines (see Figure 4.2 on the preceding page). The improvement in speed and throughput was amazing. System performance increased linearly with the number of database machines used.

In most projects, implementing a parallel database query mechanism would have required a major rewrite to the entire code base. But because we used the Tracer Bullet style of clearly defined interfaces between layers, we were able to make this radical change without affecting the layer above us. In our case, the data cruncher layer had no changes at all. We left the database access layer APIs intact but rewrote the code inside the interfaces. The new code was able to distribute the database calls across servers. From the data cruncher's point of view, everything just ran faster.

Later we found that the data cruncher layer became the next bottleneck. We were supplying the information from the data layer so fast that the data cruncher server couldn't keep up. The data crunchers became the bottleneck.

Fortunately for us, when you use this type of architecture, you can often parallelize the work across multiple data crunchers. We added more data cruncher servers and had the web server layer divide incoming requests into groups. Each group was sent to a different data cruncher (see Figure 4.3 on page 125).

We were analyzing very large data sets, but the analysis of each group was independent of the others. Since we used the same interface and gave it a smaller amount of data to analyze, the data cruncher layer didn't know anything had changed. We were able to add an arbitrary number of data cruncher servers to the system and handle as much workload as the client required.

You can't do this type of refactoring and parallelization for every application, but this example illustrates the amazing flexibility and power you get when you clearly define interfaces between different layers of your application. We were able to do major work in one layer without changing the adjacent layers.

Another important thing to note is that even though this example discusses using different servers, you don't have to do that. We use different servers in our scenario to illustrate the demarcation. The same principle applies to an application. Take, for instance, the Model-View-Controller (MVC)[3] paradigm. When you clearly define the interfaces between the logic, the data, and the graphical user interface (GUI), you free up each group to work independently. In fact, the entire purpose of using MVC is to have this type of encapsulation.

> **TIP 23**
>
> An encapsulated architecture is a scalable architecture

Selling Tracer Bullets

The benefits to the Tracer Bullet Development are enormous. However, if you're introducing the idea to your shop, you may need to sell the concept to your team mates or boss. With that in mind, we summarize the benefits to working in the Tracer Bullet paradigm.

Teams can work in parallel. Your team can work independently once the interfaces are stubbed out.

Your customer sees the "working" system earlier, and provides feedback sooner. You can demonstrate the system as soon as all the teams have their interfaces stubbed out. As you add functionality, the new features can be demonstrated immediately. Remember that the sooner the customer sees the product, the sooner they can correct any problems in

---

[3]The MVC concept is a time-tested encapsulation model. It forces clear lines of separation between the view of the data, the data model, and the controller (or logic). This idea fits in well here. If you're not familiar with MVC, you should be!

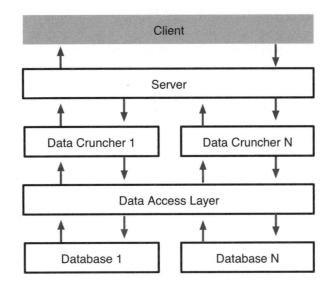

Figure 4.3: A FOUR-LAYER SYSTEM WITH MULTIPLE CRUNCHERS

your product's direction. Customers often have an idea of what they want but aren't able to clearly define the requirements for you. This type of customer needs to see a running system before they can provide you any real feedback on the product's direction. Tracer Bullet Development lets you create a running system very quickly without writing throw-away demo code.

Momentum! Never underestimate the effect morale has on productivity. Morale skyrockets when everyone is getting work done and the product is coming together.

As soon as you define your interfaces, your testing group can begin writing automated test scripts to run against them. By the time the complete product is ready to begin real testing (that's to say, all the parts have been filled in and are working), the testing team should have a suite of automated tests ready to run. The tests will change just as the interfaces did, but the framework is in place. There will be modifications, but no one will be starting from scratch. Each layer in the system can be independently validated with this type of test suite in place.

When you build a project in the Tracer Bullet paradigm, you establish a set of teams, and set up the ground rules for their interaction. You force them to interact and come to an agreement on key project points. In addition to learning to communicate with the other teams, you're allowing your teams to define the changes in the interfaces, which gives each team even more product ownership. They defined the project's interfaces originally, so they already feel significant ownership of it. Now they're refining and improving it. Consequently, everyone works harder to make their project succeed.

Getting your teams working in parallel this way leads to huge productivity gains and is a very efficient use of your development and testing time. We've worked with teams of only four developers where we all defined the interfaces for each layer together, then each of the four team members wrote one of the layers by themselves. Once the stubs were written, we had a running system.

Anytime your product stops working, you know someone has broken an interface and you can fix it quickly. You can also use this approach with larger teams with equal success. It's easy to move team members from one layer to another with this type of autonomy. Your team members already have a basic understanding of what needs to be done in adjacent layers because they helped to define the interface. If any one area falls behind, you can easily move developers from one layer to another.

The time to market on this type of development is amazing. As soon as you have a Tracer Bullet with a GUI on it, the client can see what it looks like and start giving you feedback. You can decide to ship or beta test what you have as soon as enough of the functionality is working. You don't have to wait for it "all" to be finished before your sales team starts demos because you have an end-to-end working system. You can also get feedback from customers on which features to finish next. Your development team isn't guessing about priorities because they've become "customer driven."[4] Integrating your customer into your development cycle is a huge benefit whether you're in a small or large company. In most cases, if the customer ain't happy, ain't nobody happy.

Turning the rudder is useless if a boat isn't moving. The same can be said of your development and testing groups. Once everyone is moving, it's much easier to keep them moving. TBD keeps all your teams

---

[4]For real, not just as a buzzword

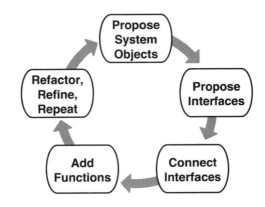

Figure 4.4: TRACER BULLET DEVELOPMENT

headed toward the same goal, while at the same time enabling each team to work independently. Each team will work by themselves but toward the common goal that all the members defined together. Your team members can see the progress when your team is moving and has momentum. Each team member is contributing to a working system that improves daily and weekly. The code you add today affects what runs today. The impact that momentum has on morale is amazing.

TIP 24

You can't steer a boat unless its moving

The Tracer Bullet Development process may not be right for every situation (though we have yet to see a project it doesn't work for). It's a very effective way to run a project that scales up to very large teams, handles projects of any size, and gives your architecture the flexibility to do amazing things. The encapsulation of functional areas, the parallel work efforts, the rapid customer feedback, and other features make it one of the more flexible and effective ways to develop software and one that you should explore for your next project. It's a very powerful and versatile tool that you should have in your toolbox.[5]

---

[5]Remember that having a tool in your toolbox doesn't mean you must use it every day. It means that the tool is available to you as needed.

How to Get Started

The best way to get started with TBD is to pick a project and try it out. Review the concept with your teammates before you get started. We'd suggest you try a smaller project first to get a feel for how TBD works.

- Define your system objects.
- Define the interfaces between them.
- Write the interface stubs.
- Make the stubs talk with each other.
- Fill in the stubs with functional code.

You're Doing It Right If...

- The entire system is always up and "running."
- Team members understand the system objects as well as "their" objects.
- Team members feel comfortable helping out with other system objects.
- You can rewrite large portions of your code base and nothing breaks.

Warning Signs

- Team members argue for hours over the "right way" to design an interface.
- The end-to-end system never actually runs end to end.
- Builds are frequently broken because interfaces were changed and the consumers didn't know.
- You have only one big honking system object.
- You have 700 itty-bitty system objects.
- The team has been working for months and the system still doesn't have compiling stubs.
- The team has had compiling stubs for months and no working features are in place.

Most people spend more time and energy going around problems than in trying to solve them.
► Henry Ford

Chapter 5

Common Problems and How to Fix Them

At this point in the book you may well be thinking, "This is all well and good, but how does it all work in real life? How the heck can I use this stuff to solve my current problem?" Have we got a chapter for you!

This chapter outlines some common problems that we've personally encountered. In each section we'll describe the problem then give an overview of our solutions. When necessary, we drill deeper, customizing the solution to fit your specific role (e.g., developer, tech lead, manager, customer). That's not to say you shouldn't read the other sections, of course. By doing so you'll gain insight on "how the other half lives." You'll also learn techniques that you can adapt to fit your role.

For example, if you don't have a role with authority, apply the management solutions by suggesting, discussing, and persuading. (Perhaps those nominally in authority could do more of that, too!)

You'll notice an underlying theme in all the sections of this chapter: taking action. This chapter isn't for those who are happy with the status quo or who have given up the fight. But if you're itching to take it on and make things better, read on.

Help! I've Inherited Legacy Code

You've inherited a legacy product that you will be maintaining and enhancing. What's the quickest way to get a handle on it? Learn to build it, automate it, and finally test it.

1. *Build it*: First, figure out how to build it, and then script that build process. This task isn't always easy, especially if the code has had only one owner. The code will often build on only one machine because it relies on the surrounding environment. Once complete, anybody can build the product on any machine. After that, it should be easy to automate the builds.

2. *Automate it*: Your goal is to automatically build and test the entire product on a clean machine with an absolute minimum of manual intervention. We didn't say *no* manual intervention; there's a balance here. Sometimes it's easier to manually install and configure a supporting piece of the environment than to write a script to do it automatically. Apps that you install only once are prime candidates (compilers, etc.). Document all the build steps and make this documentation publicly available.

3. *Test it*: Figure out what the code does, then begin testing by writing mock client tests for it (see the sidebar on page 46). Once you have the project building cleanly, you'll want to confirm that it works. In order to write the tests, you'll have to learn exactly what the product is supposed to do (no surprise there).

   Mock client tests are a good starting point: they test the broad functionality of a product because they act just as a product user would.

4. *Test it more*: Figure out the product's innards (things such as structure, flow-of-control, performance, and scalability), and write more tests for it. Unless the product is completely unused, there *will* be bugs you'll need to fix (or at least document) or enhancements you'll have to make. Normally these changes are a pretty scary thing to do to legacy code, because you're never quite sure what you're going to affect when you make a code change. But you can do this fearlessly because of the mock client tests you wrote as a safety net; they'll keep you from breaking things too badly. (You *did* write those tests, didn't you?)

Write a new test for every bug you fix and for every enhancement you add to the product. The type of test you write will depend on what you're changing (e.g., a unit test for a low-level internal change, or a mock client test for a new feature). At this point you're treating the legacy product in the same way you would any other product you support.

After you've done all this, *anybody* will be able to support this code! They'll be able to automatically build it anywhere and then confirm it's working correctly by running the automated tests on their desktop. And the automated build system will run the build and tests again in a clean environment to be sure that everything is really still working.

TIP 25

Don't change legacy code until you can test it

Testing Untestable Code

If you are a developer or tester trying to get an automated test suite set up for your product, you may find yourself in the uncomfortable position of trying to test a product that doesn't have good "hooks" for your test rigs. It's not impossible to test "untestable" code, but the effort involved in test creation and maintenance usually cancels out the benefit of the automation.

For instance, you might be trying to test an HTML page that has a lot of unnamed fields. So instead of using the "name" or "id" tags to locate a field, you count the items on the page and check the value in the fifth item. This is very difficult for someone else to understand and maintain, but the test is also very fragile. Often, changes to the page will break your test.

What's the solution? Tell your manager you want to start *test driven refactoring*. You want to start adding the simple hooks to your application that make it possible (or feasible) to do good automated testing.

First, create (or borrow) a test plan for the product. Keep the plan simple at first. Don't try to make it perfect on your first attempt. Shoot for a simple pass that exercises basic functionality.

Second, write an automated test. Make the test go as far as you can. When you get stuck, what's the least amount you can add to the product's code to get the test running? Is it just a return code to an existing API or an "id" tag for an HTML field?

Don't try to fix every problem with your first pass. Don't try to add "id" tags to every page in your product; shoot for the one page you need to get the test passing. If your test plan hits a roadblock, don't stop. Remove the part of the test plan you can't test and move on. Remember that you can also add the hard part to your next test plan.

The goal here is incremental improvement and momentum. As you make small improvements, your developers will start learning how to create testable products. As you write automated tests, you'll start learning tricks too. You'll be surprised at how much support you'll get once you've got a basic automation suite in place.

TIP 26

Use test driven refactoring to clean up untestable code

18 ▶ Features Keep Breaking

Here's a scenario that is all too common in a lot of development shops: your team sends another interim version of your product to the testing department. The next week you get a call from a tester saying that one of the main product features is broken again. This is the fifth time this has happened in the last seven internal releases. At least the tester caught it before it went out to the customer. Last time *that* happened, the customer had to revert to an earlier version of the product, and you almost lost the account.

You look at the code for the feature, and, sure enough, a bug fix you put in last month has mysteriously disappeared. You spend the rest of the day re-entering the bug fix code and spend yet another evening at work instead of doing what you had planned to do before you got that phone call.

What's the quickest way to fix this problem? Add an automated test suite (see Practice 7, *Use a Testing Harness*, on page 43). A mock client test suite (sidebar 7 on page 46) is your best choice to get the product or platform stable as quickly as possible. Mock client tests exercise the most lines of code in the least amount of time.

> TIP 27
>
> Mock client tests do the most with the least

Run the test suite automatically whenever code changes so that you know when a feature breaks (see Practice 4, *Build Automatically*, on page 31). This system will catch bugs as soon as they are reintroduced and notify the responsible developer. Now, the responsibility of fixing the problem is on the shoulders on the developer who changed the code.

Not creating an automated test suite means you depend solely on manual testing to locate bugs. This is slow and error prone. Not running the tests automatically means you are storing up potential breakages so you can fix a lot of them at the same time.

To keep your product stable, test with automated mock client tests and run the tests after every code change.

19 ▶ Tests? We Stopped Using Them

Your team has invested time into creating a set of tests that can be run automatically, but the tests just aren't used.

Maybe you don't have a testing group, and the developers are just too swamped to pick up the slack. Maybe you have testers, but they can't run the tests because they don't have the correct infrastructure installed on their machines. Little by little the tests break, but no one realizes it because nobody runs them. When somebody does try to run them, the results are meaningless because the tests no longer match the code base. Your tests have become useless.

When that happens, it's time to start again. Perhaps no one was using the tests because they weren't getting benefit from them. Normally the benefit is immediate and obvious, but there is an upfront cost to get started (or restarted) that you just have to put up with. It wasn't raining when Noah built the ark, after all.

The other problem you may face comes later in the project's life. The more tests you add, the more time it takes to run them after a compile. At some point, you may not be able to run all the tests every time. Which tests should you pick to run continuously? Choose those tests that best exercise the code that is being actively developed. When you notice that a test is broken in nightly or weekly builds, move it to the CI test suite so it can be run more frequently. We discuss this type of targeted testing in more detail in the *Use a Testing Harness* section (see Practice 7, *Use a Testing Harness*, on page 43).

> **TIP 28**
>
> Continuously test changing code

If need be, run your CI system on more than one machine so that you can run your tests in parallel. This can run an hour's worth of tests in fifteen minutes by running them in parallel on four machines. It's also a great way to get cross-platform test coverage.

At one small startup we worked with, the same CI system ran on Windows, Linux, and Solaris. Each platform had the same test suite running, ensuring that the product still ran on each platform. Even though our developers worked primarily on a single platform, we continually tested on every platform on which we shipped the product.

Do this, and you'll avoid the end-of-the-release-cycle scramble to fix platform-specific bugs.

Until you have a CI environment that builds your product after each code change, you won't be testing your code often enough. Even a daily build is not sufficient. Look at it this way: a team of developers can change a *lot* of code in a day. Whenever your team runs the test suite, they look at the test results, isolate the failures, and then figure out which code changes caused the failures. This is easy if there have been only a few code changes. Pretty much anybody on the team can do it.

However, if you build and test only after a large amount of code is changed, it gets much harder. If you wait too long, the only person who can match failed tests to code is someone who is intimately familiar with the product, its code, and the tests. This job usually falls to a senior team member. Instead of adding features or fixing bugs, they're tracing other developers' code.

That's not very efficient, and that's why a good CI system will make the entire team more productive.

But It Works for Me!

Have you ever reported a bug and received the answer, "It works for me!" Worse, have you ever received a bug report, tried to reproduce it, and said this yourself? To be blunt, no one cares if it works for you. Your customers, your testers, and anyone who uses your product cares only if it works for them. When bugs are reported, never stop at "It works for me." It *doesn't* work for somebody else, or it wouldn't have been reported in the first place.

If you can't reproduce a bug on your own machine, the build machine is your insurance policy. Use it to verify bugs that you can't reproduce on your workstation. Once you duplicate the bug on the build machine, figure out what's different on your system. You might have already fixed the bug! Or you might have to add something to the shipping product (or its environment) so your product works everywhere. Once you've duplicated the bug, craft a test to expose it, and then run the test on the clean box. If you write the test carefully, you can even send it into the field to see if the customer can duplicate your results.

Of course, if you can not reproduce the bug on the build machine either, then perhaps the customer has a configuration problem on their own machine. Start asking questions about the environment they've set up. When you find the difference that causes the bug, either change your code to support that difference or gently but firmly tell the user to fix their configuration.

TIP 29

It has to work for everyone

21 ▶ It Hurts When I Integrate Code

Do you hate compiling your product's code base? After you've updated your local code tree from the source code management system, does it take you hours to reconcile it with everybody else's changes? Do you tend to "protect" the code on your machine by merging with the rest of the team only as a last resort? Is the term *code integration* considered a dirty word in your group? Sadly, you're not alone.

One shop we worked in was the poster child for this problem. They had only a dozen developers, but team members would go months without committing or updating code. If it happened that a developer had to build the product, they would first check out the code tree and try to compile it. When the compile failed, the hapless developer (we'll call him Hal) would print out the compile errors and try to identify who was working in the problem areas. One by one, each developer would get a visit from poor Hal who would request they fix the compile problems in their area. After each developer fixed a problem area, Hal would update his code tree and try again. Each iteration of this process took about half a day per developer. So with twelve developers, it routinely took Hal a week before he had code that would even compile. By the time all of Hal's issues had been addressed, another developer would have committed bad code, and Hal would have to start again.

How do you keep code integration from becoming an ongoing nightmare?

You'll run into two types of problems. The first problem happens when two team members edit the same file or files that depend on each other, and the result doesn't compile. A classic example of this occurs when a method signature changes. The method `loginUser` used to take one string, and now it requires two. Any code that uses the old signature will no longer compile.

The second problem is more insidious—the code compiles but doesn't work anymore. For example, Joe decides that the integer variable `SystemStatus` should contain a return code, while Cathy has started using `SystemStatus` to track what part of the program is active. If Joe and Cathy commit their code with these incompatible uses of the same `SystemStatus` variable, it will break code for both of them.

The longer you wait to integrate your code, the greater the chance that one of these conflicts will happen. The longer you wait, the more code you (and other team members) will edit. As the lines of edited code increase, the number of collisions will increase as well. The higher the number of collisions, the more painful the merge will be. The solution is simple: integrate your code more often to reduce collisions and simplify merges.

Use a CI system (see Practice 4, *Build Automatically*, on page 31). The CI system will compile all the product's code after every code commit and can automatically test the product after a successful build. So you can catch both types of integration problems without lifting a finger. (It also gives tech leads an easy place to check on developers to see who hasn't integrated their code with the team for a while.)

Tip 30

Integrate often, and build and test continuously

▶22 Can't Build the Product Reliably

We once worked in a shop that had to build their product three to five times in a row to get one good build. This had been going on for so long that the development team considered this normal. To build, a developer ran a series of scripts (generated by their IDE), intermingled with manual steps. Nobody understood what the build scripts did. Instead of figuring it out, their excuse was, "Our product is just that complicated."

We spent half a day creating a completely automated script that built the entire product from scratch. Unless the code wouldn't compile, the build always worked. Everyone was amazed! But it really wasn't that difficult. We first assumed that the build could be automated, and then we found a scripting tool that was appropriate for the language they were using. And the tool came with enough sample code snippets that we had to write very little original code to get it all working.

Why are your builds unreliable? Perhaps the process is complicated enough that it's easy for you to miss a step, it's easy to execute the steps out of order, or there's a circular dependency in the build process.[1] Scripting your build will solve this problem because scripts execute steps consistently. Once your script is in place, you will generate builds the same way every time. The less obvious reason may be that you don't clearly understand your build process. By creating a build script, you'll be forced to understand the steps precisely.

Besides increasing reliability, automated builds add a professional finish to your product, ease the transition for new team members, and let you easily use a CI system. See Practice 4, *Build Automatically*, on page 31 for more benefits and hints, as well as *The Pragmatic Programmer*'s section on *Ubiquitous Automation*[HT00].

---

[1]A depends on B, but B depends on A, so it takes a few rounds to get it all sorted out. This is usually an indication of a design flaw in your code.

> ∖∕╱ **Joe Asks...**
> ⁀⁀
> ⁀   **What If I Don't Have Any Customers?**
>
> If you're not a manager or a team lead, don't assume that
> this section doesn't apply to you. No matter how well insulated
> they are from the outside world, developers have customers
> too: their managers. Don't you want your managers to be your
> raving fans? Then treat them like customers.

23 ▶ Customers Are Unhappy

To properly manage your customers, find out what they want, and then deliver it to them. You'll know you've succeeded when they become your raving fans. Simple, huh? Well, figuring out what a customer *really* wants is often the most difficult part of a project.

Get the customer to work alongside you to help define the product while managing their expectations about what's possible and what's not. Don't just get their input at the beginning of the project; keep in touch throughout the development process. Customer feedback keeps you from building the wrong product, one that no one wants. This also makes your customers feel like co-owners of the product. The product moves from being "yours" to "ours." In the end you have a partner instead of a critic.

So how do you communicate the project status to the customer? One of the best ways is to create a live system that can be used for demonstrations as early as possible, even if the feature set is incomplete. This is true whether the product has a GUI or is a set of application programming interfaces (APIs). To provide a live system early in the development cycle, use Tracer Bullet Development (see Section 4, *Tracer Bullet Development*, on page 105). Every time your team completes a new feature, add it to the demo program so the customer can see it and give you feedback.

> ⌐ TIP 31 ⌐
> Deliver live demos early and often

How do you communicate with the customer between releases of the demo? Encourage the customer to check The List as often as possible, and keep it up-to-date so they can see it change. Invite the customer into your development world so that they can see your direction and your problems. A customer is more likely to accept a delay if they understand what caused it. Also, encourage them to suggest changes to The List. If they don't like the way the project is going, they should ask for you to change it. After all, they're paying the bills. If they frequently communicate their needs and your team continually adjusts the product to meet them, then the end result should make everyone happy.

24 ▶ ## You've Got a Rogue Developer

Every shop has at least one developer who seems to be on a different page from the rest of the team. No matter how often he breaks things, he is sure that he is on the right track and everyone else must be wrong. How can you keep this loose cannon on-task and productive?

This particular problem can be solved only by the manager. If you are a developer, it's not your job to rein in your teammates (and beatings in the parking lot are generally frowned upon in most jurisdictions). If you are a customer, you can drive features and stability, but individual developers are not issues that you should personally interfere with. Leave this to the development manager.

The Manager's Point of View

If you're the manager, there are a lot of things you can do to keep rogue developers in check without driving them out of the group. Let's look at a few of the ways you can harness their energy:

- Daily meetings keep these developers from getting too far afield by keeping them accountable on a frequent basis (see Practice 12, *Coordinate and Communicate Every Day*, on page 78). By meeting as a group daily to review what is being worked on, you can correct their course every day. You still might lose half a day's work from this individual, but you won't lose a week, a month, or a quarter. Each day the rogue has to report what they've done, what they intend to do, and the problems they've had. If you notice from day to day that what actually got done doesn't match yesterday's to-do items, then ask about it during the daily meetings.

We once worked with a developer who loved to refactor code, and he never let a lack of understanding of its function get in his way! When he finished his currently assigned task, he would start refactoring any code that he had happened across during his work. For instance, if he invoked a class that had a statistical algorithm in it, he would refactor it even though he had no idea what the code was doing or why. He was "cleaning it up. . . ."; unfortunately, he usually broke it as well. He always formatted it nicely, but it usually didn't run quite the same way it had before. Whenever random bugs popped up in the system, we would check the source code repository history to see if this guy had been there, and, usually, he had.

Once we realized what was going on, we made sure at each daily meeting that he had enough work assigned to him to last until the next day. Sometimes he would finish early and go wandering off through the code, but generally, the daily meeting was all we needed to keep him in check. We just had to make sure his daily assignment was actually enough to keep him busy.

In general, rogues aren't malicious. They're trying to help out by going above and beyond what you asked them to do. More guidance and oversight can often defuse the problem. You don't need to exercise this level of oversight with every team member, just the wanderers.

- Using The List is another good way to rein in rogues (see Practice 10, *Work from The List*, on page 57). If everyone uses their own copy of The List to drive their work, they find it hard to justify why they worked on an item that wasn't on The List. This works best if you as their manager help fill out The List of each of your team members.

  Quite often rogues are just trying to help. Granted, their idea of helping usually comes from a unique point of view (probably not yours). By using The List, you make it clear to the rogue which tasks *you* consider important.

  You do not have to limit the rogue's tasks to product features. Instead of just overloading them with work, let them play from time to time. If they want to refactor, let them do it on nonproduction code. Or let them invent some new tool, research a new programming technique, and then teach it to the team. But be sure to put these tasks on The List to keep the rogue accountable.

  Occasionally you will find a rogue who's arrogant enough that they don't care what their assigned tasks are. They are sure that the manager or tech lead is irrelevant and doesn't know as much as they do. No matter how clearly you lay out a path of work, they will ignore it. There's really only one thing to do: document the rogue's behavior, and terminate them for insubordination. In most cases, just starting the documentation process will jolt the rogue into line. And if it doesn't, you're going to be better off without them.

- Code reviews are another great way to keep a rogue developer under control (see Practice 13, *Review All Code*, on page 88). When you review the rogue's code, they have to explain to you what they did and why. No more silent, and perhaps unnoticed, code commits. You'll see each page (and we hope, each line) of code. If you find their work is not directly related to an item on The List, then don't approve the code commit. If you have a particularly strong-willed (or stubborn) individual, have a senior team member do their code reviews, not someone they can bully into signing off on a bad code change.

- Use automatic code change notifications (see Practice 14, *Send Code Change Notifications*, on page 98). This lets you audit exactly what code was committed and for what reason. Scan the rogue's notifications and see if they are working in files or packages that have nothing to do with their assigned tasks.

- Start using a CI system (see Practice 4, *Build Automatically*, on page 31). Even if the rogue checks in code that hasn't yet been reviewed, or doesn't mail around a complete code diff, they cannot escape the watchful eye of a virtual build monitor! Every time someone checks in code, the CI system builds the project and runs the tests, and then it sends mail to the project contacts with a report on what files were touched. If rogue has altered files that shouldn't have been touched, you'll know.

  Using a CI system to keep an eye on team members should be a last resort. This type of a situation is rarely the motivation behind using a CI system but can be necessary if you do have rogue developers breaking code. A CI system solves a wide variety of problems, but this is probably one of the most extreme.

As you can see, you have a variety of tools to deal with rogue developers. Use them, and in most cases it will be fairly straightforward to keep rogue developers on-task. Eventually, they'll build up good work habits, and you won't have to watch them so closely.

To summarize, do the following:

- Use daily meetings to correct a rogue developer's course.
- Hold the rogue developer to the tasks on The List.
- Use code reviews and automatic code change notifications to track a rogue developer's work.
- Use CI as a last resort to monitor a rogue developer's work.

25 ▶ Your Manager Is Unhappy

How do you keep your manager happy? It comes down to one word: *communication.* Make sure your manager always understands what you are doing and why. What about productivity, you ask? You can be the most productive worker in the world, but if your manager doesn't know it, it won't matter. So the real question is how can you effectively communicate with your manager?

- Use The List (see Practice 10, *Work from The List*, on page 57), even if it's just personally. It helps you organize your work and understand why you're doing it. If you don't understand it yourself, there is no way you can describe it to your manager. If you try, you'll sound unorganized and unintelligent. With The List in place and up-to-date, however, you can tell your manager what's going on at a moment's notice.

  Don't prepare The List in a vacuum; periodically get your managers to review it. They'll safety-check your work plans and priorities. If they want you to work in another area, they'll tell you. If you're working exactly where you're supposed to, you've reinforced that warm, fuzzy feeling you want your manager to have about you. In either case they'll feel good about your work because they helped set the direction.

- Keep your manager up-to-date with your progress. If you can't meet face to face at least weekly, send an email with a high-level summary of what you are doing. Don't make this a long, drawn-out, detailed report (unless your manager asks for it). Keep it short and to the point. For example, say, "I helped Trev with an install issue on AIX" instead of "Trev and I worked for four hours trying to get the Gizmo installed on AIX 5.1. As it turns out, our installer works fine on 5.2, but 5.1 had an issue with the number of file handles you can have open. After reviewing the problem with John and Mark, we finally decided that it was in fact a low-level issue with our installer code, and we got in touch with Steve to fix it." The first version is a concise summary. The second is too long-winded. If necessary, split the status report into two sections: a summary of everything you've done at the beginning and then more details on individual items after that.

TIP 32
Publicize what you're doing and why

What If My Boss Drops in Every Hour for a Status Update?

If you work for a micromanager who drops in three times a day to check on a six-month project, just show them The List (see Practice 10, *Work from The List*, on page 57). Point out that the same task that wasn't finished an hour ago still isn't finished. Every time they visit you, use The List as a visual aid. This way you can train them to just walk in and look at The List instead of interrupting your work all the time.

Another tack you can take is to encourage your manager to hold Daily Meetings (see Practice 12, *Coordinate and Communicate Every Day*, on page 78) and report your status there. When managers get regular updates at specific times, they tend not to interrupt you as often (especially if you point out just how much the interruptions hurt your productivity).

26 ▶ Team Doesn't Work Well Together

You have a group of developers who are on the same team, but they don't talk to each other, they don't eat lunch together, and they never hang out at the proverbial watercooler talking about last night's game. How do you get this group of isolated strangers to actually interact with each other instead of hiding in their offices?

- If you don't already have them, start daily meetings (see Practice 12, *Coordinate and Communicate Every Day*, on page 78) or get your manager to do so. At a daily meeting, everyone talks. Just this simple forced interaction will draw out shy individuals in an amazing way.

- Have team members review each other's code before commits (see Practice 13, *Review All Code*, on page 88). By mandating code reviews (with rotating reviewers), you force the team to talk with each other and discuss their work. They share opinions and learn about each other's technical style and capabilities. If you're a developer, then start a movement by getting other team members to review *your* code. Be open and friendly, and don't get defensive no matter what happens. And be sure to spread around how helpful it was and how much more productive you are. Make code reviews seem attractive enough, and the rest of the group will hold them, too.

- Meet once a week for lunch. A regular informal lunch is a great way to build friendships. You'll learn a lot about your teammates just by watching them decide which restaurant to eat at!

> TIP 33
> Face time builds teamwork

Most team-building exercises are isolated encounters, such as retreat weekends or workshops. We don't discount such events outright but simply remind you that building teamwork is an ongoing, day-by-day exercise. If you choose to have team-building events, be sure to supplement them with everyday actions. Ongoing, day-to-day team-building habits work the best. And the next time you add a new member to the team, they'll fit right in without much effort.

Can't Get "Buy-in" on Essential Points

You can't get team members, management, or stakeholders to participate in vital project practices or processes. You've preached, you've cajoled, you've demonstrated, you've even mandated (if you're in a position of authority), and nobody is doing it right. It might be time to give up on this group of people and find others who are more willing to listen. But before you bolt, try some of these suggestions.

The Manager's Point of View

Sell the new practice or process to the team; don't just dictate policy. Don't just preach it; demonstrate it. People respond to a working example more often than to a lecture, no matter how good the concept. This means that you'll have to learn it first yourself, or pick one of your self-starters to learn it. You want to have an in-house expert that the rest of the team can go to for questions, problems, and general "Am I doing this right?" hand-holding. Pick someone who is patient with newbies, communicates well, can dig for answers to the hard questions, and isn't already working full-time on a critical part of the project. And make sure the rest of the team respects them. Don't pick a third-string team member just because they're free right now. Your team will respect the new practice only as much as they respect the person championing it.

Make it easy for your team to change. It's hard enough to learn anything new in a comfortable, forgiving environment. Don't make it harder by shoehorning it into an already too-full schedule or demanding immediate perfection. Give them extra time to come up to speed on the new practice. Get them books or training if they need it. And choose the right time to introduce the new practice or process (see Practice 28, *The New Practice Didn't Help*, on page 151). (Hint: three days before the product ship date is *not* the right time!)

Show your team how these practices benefit them personally. Appeal to their enlightened self-interest (in other words, what's in it for *them*?) "You should do this because it will improve product quality" won't motivate the majority of people. "Use this, and you'll be able to go home at 5 p.m. every day" works much better. And don't be above providing incentives. Set a goal, and then offer the team a reward for meeting it. It could be as small as a box of doughnuts or as big as a major bonus for all concerned. But give the group something concrete to shoot for.

The Internet: The World's Biggest Training Manual

Don't have much money in the budget for training? Then point your team at the Internet, and turn them loose. These days there's more information about *anything* on the Internet than anywhere else, and most of it is free. (Of course, you can't believe everything you find there; take what you find with a grain of salt.) So don't limit your team's access to the Internet. Sure, they might surf some non-work-related sites, but the good stuff they find will more than make up for it.

In the end, if this team doesn't want to move forward, replace them with people who do. Give your team every chance to adopt the new practice. If they simply won't do it and they simply can't get the job done without it, then move them aside and find better people. If you're stuck with these people and the project is going to fail, then you may well have no choice but to bolt. Hard words. But remember this: a captain who goes down with the ship usually finds it hard to get another command. . . .

The Developer's Point of View

Most of what we said to managers also applies if you're a member of the team. You don't have a manager's authority, but that doesn't count for much in this situation anyway. Sell the practice; don't preach it. Use it, become an expert, and then *show* the rest of the team how well it works for you. Look for specific situations where the practice can help a teammate out of a jam, and then offer your help. (You could just go home at 5 p.m. instead, but your team probably won't think much of you after that.) Again, if your team refuses to learn a project-saving practice, then move on to greener pastures. At least you tried.

The Customer's Point of View

First, realize that you don't have a lot of say in the internal practices of the development team (and you really don't want any). It won't matter to you how the team works as long as they deliver a good product. The practices you're interested in are the ones that let you discover and solve project problems as early and as quickly as possible.

Secondly, communication and feedback are the keys. Communicate early and often with the team, and give them prompt and detailed feedback on everything you get from them. Of course, this assumes that you actually *do* get something from them. Set up the project so that the team provides you with frequent demos you can try out for yourself. Demos are much better than documentation: demos are real, and documentation is just talk. If the demos don't meet your expectations (or if you don't receive them at all), you'll have to get more involved.

So how do you get the development team to change its ways? Here are some suggestions:

- Document in detail what's lacking in the demos, and then make sure the next demo fixes the problems. If it doesn't, start requiring write-ups of how the team will respond to the problems you find.

- Bring in an expert to work with the team. Get somebody who can teach them better practices and will monitor their progress.

- If things get bad enough, renegotiate the contract to *require* them to use better practices, and then closely monitor their progress. But that's really a last resort.

Finally, if it's clear that the team won't do what it takes to deliver the product you need, then find a team that will. Don't throw good money after bad waiting for the team to miraculously improve. Cut your losses and find a better team.

28 ▶ The New Practice Didn't Help

We've talked all through this book about "standing on the shoulders of giants." The best way to do that is to learn the practices that the giants are using and use them yourself. There's always room for improvement in any software shop, so always be on the lookout for better practices that will provide that improvement.

When Not to Introduce a Practice

It seems strange to start here, doesn't it? But many shops add new practices and process when they're not necessary or at a bad time when they'll be disruptive to critical work. They end up causing more problems than they solve. The first question you should ask yourself whenever you're thinking about adding any practice should be, "Is now a good time to do it?"

Don't try to introduce a new practice or process if there isn't a problem that needs fixing. Never introduce a change because it's "the right thing to do." Instead, identify the actual problems in your shop, and then figure out how to fix them. Before you know it, you'll have a smoothly running shop because you've fixed only what's broken.

TIP 34
Only fix what needs fixing

Be creative when thinking about problems and fixes. "There's more than one way to do it"[2] applies to more than just Perl programs! There are lots of ways to successfully run a software shop. No set of practices and no process will always work for every team on every project.

You also need to think about what else is going on in your shop before you introduce a new practice. Three days before a major release is probably not a good time to change your current process. Your team will probably not take kindly to any distractions when they're frantically trying to get the product out the door. A much better time would be a week or so after the product ships, so the team can "catch their breath" before considering the change. So choose a time to introduce the practice that will minimize disruptions to critical activities.

---

[2]The Perl mantra, noted at the bottom of the Perl man page

> **TIP 35**
>
> Disruptive "best practices" aren't

And of course, make sure the practice or process you're considering will actually *improve* things. If it won't make things run faster and more efficiently, your team won't (and shouldn't!) adopt it. As far as they're concerned, "If it lets me go home at 5 p.m., I'll do it."

How to Introduce a New Practice

Once you've decided to add a new practice to your repertoire, how do you go about doing it effectively? There are two main things you've got to do: *demonstrate* and *persuade*. Accomplish these two goals, and you'll have a group of raving fans in no time.

You've got to get buy-in from several groups of people. First and foremost are the people who will actually be *practicing* the new practice, namely, your team. If they aren't excited about it, it won't matter if anyone else is. How many stories have you heard about companies that have mandated from the top down new ways of doing things? And how many of these mandates have produced lasting change for the better? (Answer: not many. Think Total Quality Management, ISO-9000, and the like.)

Conversely, how many times have you heard about technologies and practices that have been brought in at the grassroots level, which then sweep through a group, company, or even industry like wildfire? (Think UNIX vs. mainframes, PCs vs. UNIX, agile development vs. the Waterfall software development model.)

> **TIP 36**
>
> Innovate from the bottom up

So how do get your team excited about this new idea? Remember we talked earlier about demonstrating? Show them the process or tool; don't just tell them about it. In particular, show them how well it works, especially in comparison with the old way of doing things.

If you know a "raving fan" who has actually used this practice to good effect, bring them in and have them show the group how well it has worked for them. Even better, use it yourself. Build up evidence about how much more productive and efficient you are, and then tell your team about it. You probably won't have to do much talking because the team has probably already noticed how much better you're doing! The key is to *prove* that this new-fangled idea is everything you say it is.

TIP 37

Show, don't just tell

Persuading your team to use this new practice is critical. That's not to say that you can completely ignore your management, however. Getting buy-in from your manager makes introducing a practice easier. Your manager can persuade those team members on the fence about the idea to give it a try and can act as a shield from the rest of the company. Such shielding can give your group time to figure out the best way to implement the practice. And obviously, it's easier to work out a change in your group when you don't have to hide what you're doing.

If you can't get management buy-in, don't let that dissuade you from adopting a practice, especially if the team is excited about it. Treat it like a "stealth practice," and use it quietly but fully. Practices like code reviews don't require management buy-in to be effective. You can use them without anyone outside your team being aware that you are having code reviews. You can set up a CI system on your own box and share the results with your team. After you've gotten some experience with the practice, show the practice, along with the associated benefits, to management.

TIP 38

Cultivate management buy-in

There's No Automated Testing

Once you've worked in a shop with an automated test suite, you'll never want to work without it again. But what if you find yourself in a shop that doesn't have it? What's the easiest way to introduce automated testing to your shop?

The biggest complaint that people have about automated tests is that maintaining them is too much trouble. If they're run infrequently, they tend to break between runs. The more time between runs, the more tests break. Leave them broken for too long, and fixing them turns into a maintenance nightmare.

So let's address this issue first. Before you start writing and committing tests, be sure that you have a CI system in place (see Practice 4, *Build Automatically*, on page 31). Set it up to run the tests every time the code changes.

When the tests are run every time someone pushes code, and that person is notified, the tests can be fixed as soon as they break. Fixing one test here and two tests there is much easier than fixing a gazillion tests just before the product ships!

If you have test code that you've been running manually, port it to the CI system. Unless the test code is a real mess, you'll get more tests in the system sooner this way. Try porting a few tests to see how easy it is. If it looks like the port will be more trouble than it's worth, then give up the effort and create a new test suite.

Next, write your tests using mock client testing (see the sidebar on page 46) to get the maximum return for each test. It's too late for you to write a unit test for every method in your code. Mock client tests are more efficient because a single test exercises a lot of code.

Identify the tests to write using defect-driven testing (see the sidebar on page 44). This will let you add tests where they can do the most good. Only add a test if there is an active bug there right now. This means that any test you add will address the most current issues in your code, and you'll get the maximum possible benefit out of every test.

TIP 39

Test where the bugs are

We're Junior Developers, With No Mentor

You're one of a small number of senior developers in a shop with a lot of junior or mid-level developers. How do you leverage your experience as a master craftsman to teach the apprentices without suffering a nervous breakdown from overwork?

First, get your team lead or manager to start holding daily meetings with your team (see Practice 12, *Coordinate and Communicate Every Day*, on page 78). Make the daily meeting a nonthreatening forum where the junior team members can discuss their problems without explicitly asking for help. Then you can share solutions without meeting with every team member individually.

Second, introduce code reviews (see Practice 13, *Review All Code*, on page 88), and make sure you or one of the other seniors attend each review. A code review is a great place for one-on-one mentoring and interaction, so do more than just make sure the code runs correctly. Tutor the junior member on more wide-ranging topics such as algorithm efficiency and coding style.

Over time the junior members will pick up good habits from their elders and will start acting suspiciously like senior programmers themselves.

31 ▶ We're on a "Death March" Project

You're on a Death March project when you're working long hours and long weeks, usually because management imposes unreasonable deadlines. Ten-to-twelve-hour workdays and weekend work become the norm. But you're doing it for the good of the project, right? It's the difference between success and failure! Well...

First, recognize that a Death March is not a good way to write software. You become mentally fatigued and make dumb mistakes when you work long hours. You take shortcuts in the tenth hour of a twelve-hour day. You are miserable when you're putting in eighty hours a week, and the product is still substandard.

Many books can already tell you how to survive a Death March [You99]. Let's look at taming it instead.

First, create a new project schedule. Use The List (Practice 10, *Work from The List*, on page 57), and put time estimates on each item. Be sure these are realistic time estimates, not Death March estimates. Work with your tech lead to get the priorities correct and in line with management.

Second, with the time estimates on The List, put together a time line for the project. (This works whether it is your personal version of The List or the group's.) Publicize this schedule. Put it on your white board or your web site. Often schedule makers create time lines simply because they don't understand the work involved. Help them understand.

Your new schedule probably blows right past the existing deadlines; that's okay. You want to get an accurate idea of where the project will actually be on a given date, not fabricate a time line to support an artificial end game.

Once you have a better idea of how much work you can reasonably accomplish, show the time line to your manager. Tell them you think the project is in trouble. Management may not be happy with your predictions, but happiness isn't the goal. Try to show them that if the schedule doesn't match reality, the schedule can't be met (although in some situations, it may be decided to keep the bad schedule for other reasons).

Now at this point, you've got two choices: move the date or drop the features. (Or quit. Make that three choices.) The choice your team

About Deadlines

"I love deadlines. I especially love the swooshing sound they make as they go flying by."—Douglas Adams

makes will depend on what's more important: the ship date or the features. If you decide to move the date, keep an active copy of The List so that nobody can add features without adjusting the time line again.

You've now shown (we hope) your ability to organize and make a reasonable plan. If your plans turn out to be accurate, you might get tapped to help avoid the problem on the next project.

Features Keep Creeping In

Unless you are extremely good at predicting the future, your initial version of The List will not make everybody happy for long. You'll get suggestions for new features that will make "all the difference" in the success of your product. How do you decide whether to add these features, and how do you convince those whose suggestions you rejected that you made the right decision?

When someone requests a new feature, look at the tasks your team is currently implementing. Is there time to implement the new feature before the next delivery? Will the new feature work with the already-scheduled features? Will it even make sense in the context of the planned product?

If the answer to these questions is "yes," then by all means add the feature to The List. Decide how important it is compared to the other features, and assign it a priority and a developer to implement it. Then sleep easy because the feature has its proper place on The List.

However, if the answer to one or more of these questions is "no," then don't add the feature, regardless of the pressure you get from the requester. Instead, gently but firmly use The List to explain why you won't implement the feature. If the requester is a rational individual and open to reasoned argument, this shouldn't be difficult. If the requester won't take no for an answer, then make a polite excuse to get back to work. Continuing the discussion at this point is a waste of time.

At one small company where we worked there were several people who would regularly come up with new features for the product. Sometimes these features made sense, but often they fell under the category of "fluff" or were simply not important enough to reassign developers to implement. This was a startup company, and money was tight. A slipped delivery meant that the company didn't get the money it needed to make payroll. We had The List on the white board in the developers' office (yes, we were so small that all the developers were in one office!) where it was visible and prioritized. After a short discussion it was usually clear why we wouldn't be implementing the "feature of the day."

33 ▶ We're Never Done

Suppose your company sells a complex software product, and you're the leader of the team that will develop the next version. How do you decide what to do? Use The List to break down the product into individual features (see Practice 10, *Work from The List*, on page 57). You'll know your project is finished when all the features on The List are implemented and are working well together (of course, feature integration should be one of the tasks on The List!).

We once came into a company that had been working on a product for nearly two years. This product was in permanent demo mode, because nobody knew how to finish the first release. Stakeholders would request different (and often conflicting) requirements on a regular basis, usually because of the latest conversation with a potential customer. The code was a conglomeration of half-finished features that worked just well enough to show at a demo. None were far enough along to be considered complete, and several had been de-emphasized but not removed from the code repository. The first thing we did was to develop a picture of the product by creating The List of features it contained. At that point we were able to figure out what features to finish for the first product release, which finally shipped a few months later.

The following are guidelines for your feature list:

- Break down any item with a time estimate of more than one week into subtasks. It's okay to have a top-level task that takes weeks or months, but that estimate is just a guess unless you back it up with estimates for its subtasks.

- Any item that takes less than one day is too small. If an item can be scheduled for a time period shorter than a day, that item is probably too low-level for The List.

- A single customer example (or *use case* or *scenario*) can involve multiple features in The List. Don't try to force an entire example into a low-level item in The List; break it into subtasks.

- Add priorities to the items on The List, then stick with them. Don't work on a priority-two item while there are priority-one items that are unfinished. But feel free to change those priorities as it becomes necessary.

- Assign specific people to each feature on The List. You can do it on the fly (as one person finishes a task, they "sign up" for another), or you can assign them all up front, and then change them as necessary. It depends on how your team works best.

- Be flexible. Use change to your advantage. Changing The List means that you're improving and refining it, that you're getting customer feedback, and that you're matching The List with the real needs of your customers.

It's like the story about an airplane that was grounded. When the passengers in the airport heard about it, they all groaned, except for one man. His happy explanation caught everyone else off guard. He said, "Look, if the airplane is grounded, either there's something wrong with the pilot, the plane, or the weather. Anyway you slice it, I'd rather be down here than up there if something is wrong!" Think about The List in the same way. If you change the features, it's because they were wrong before. In effect you were building the wrong product. As frustrating as the change is now, it's worse to finish the product and then have to throw it all away and begin again.

> **TIP 40**
> The list is a living document. Change is life

The Developer's Point of View

If your team doesn't use The List for tracking features, you can still use it yourself. Keep The List on your white board, and list everything you're working on. Then ask your tech lead to help set your priorities. If they won't help, then set the priorities yourself, but don't stress over what's more important. That's the tech lead's job. Now your work is visible, transparent, and auditable.

The Manager's Point of View

Make The List the core tool of your project management. Set your team's work assignments directly from The List. Your List may contain top-level items, low-level items, or a mix of both. Be flexible. Be sure that The List is prioritized. Otherwise, your team will have to guess at what matters most and will, as a general rule, choose the coolest or easiest features before the ones that are necessary (and coincidentally, difficult and boring).

Don't just remove an item from The List after it's finished. Keep a copy of completed features (along with dates, priority, and assigned developer) to use as your audit trail. When you're asked, "Why didn't feature X go in?" or "What features did go in?" The List will give you the answers.

> **TIP 41**
>
> If it's not on The List, it's not part of the project

After the product ships, don't forget to revisit missed goal dates on The List. Examining schedule misses will improve your future forecasting skills. Don't settle for "It slipped." Insist on details but not a witch-hunt; you want to find out why it slipped so you can fix it. Those who ignore history are doomed to repeat it, after all. Learn the lessons, or repeat the failure.

The Customer's Point of View

Ask for a copy of The List from your development group. Don't settle for top-level tasks only. You don't have to spend days reading it all, but you want to know that your development team has a detailed grasp of work scope. If the team misses some milestones, sit down with the development managers and The List and figure out why. This will give you a good picture of exactly what is going on and will help the development teams stay organized. (If they aren't using The List, this request should get them started!)

If the features on The List don't match your priorities, you need to provide that feedback quickly. If you don't ask for what you want, you certainly won't get it. And every day you wait is another day of wasted development time. Remember that the longer a team works on a feature set, the more frustrated they are when it changes. So review The List as soon as you get it. Make the time. Send the feedback (positive or negative). Timely feedback is an amazingly motivating thing. Don't squander the opportunity.

> **TIP 42**
>
> Always give feedback fast

Appendix A

Tip Summary

1. Choose your habits
2. Stay in the sandbox
3. If you need it, check it in
4. Script builds on day one
5. Any machine can be a build machine
6. Build continuously
7. Test continuously
8. Avoid collective memory loss
9. Exercise your product—automate your tests
10. Use a common, flexible test harness
11. Use the best tool for the job
12. Use open formats to integrate tools
13. Keep critical path technologies familiar
14. Work to The List
15. Let a tech lead
16. Use daily meetings for frequent course corrections
17. It's okay to say "later"
18. Always review all code
19. The goal is software, not compliance
20. Architect as a group
21. If production uses it, you should too
22. Solve the hardest problems first
23. An encapsulated architecture is a scalable architecture
24. You can't steer a boat unless its moving
25. Don't change legacy code until you can test it

26. Use test driven refactoring to clean up untestable code
27. Mock client tests do the most with the least
28. Continuously test changing code
29. It has to work for everyone
30. Integrate often, and build and test continuously
31. Deliver live demos early and often
32. Publicize what you're doing and why
33. Face time builds teamwork
34. Only fix what needs fixing
35. Disruptive "best practices" aren't
36. Innovate from the bottom up
37. Show, don't just tell
38. Cultivate management buy-in
39. Test where the bugs are
40. The list is a living document. Change is life
41. If it's not on The List, it's not part of the project
42. Always give feedback fast

Source Code Management

Source Code Management (SCM) programs (also generically known as *version control* systems) keep track of your code and the changes you make to it. In addition, a good SCM associates specific versions of the code with important milestones, e.g., a product release.

What's Available:

CVS...http://www.cvshome.org
A free, open-source client-server SCM. Does everything you need, but the command-line interface is a bit arcane. CVS is used by companies large and small all over the world.

Subversion...........................http://subversion.tigris.org
The self-avowed replacement for CVS, it does most of what CVS does, plus a lot more. Like CVS, it's open-source and free.

MS Visual SourceSafe...
...http://msdn.microsoft.com/vstudio/previous/ssafe
Microsoft's SCM, it's integrated with a lot of their development tools and IDEs. If your shop paid for Microsoft's development tools, you've probably already paid for SourceSafe and have a license waiting to be used.

BitKeeper....................................http://www.bitkeeper.com
BitKeeper is a commercial product that the Linux kernel developers used for several years, and they have reported a significant increase in productivity as a result.

Key Concepts:

Repository
>   Where the source code is stored.

Workspace
>   Your local copy of the source code on your machine. You check code out of the repository into your workspace, work on it for awhile, and then check it back into the repository.

Client
>   The program you run on your machine that interfaces with the repository through the server.

Server
>   The program that sits in front of the repository and deals with the clients.

Branches
>   You branch a project so that you can have multiple development paths with that project. For example, one branch of a project would be used for bug fixes on the current version, and another branch would be used to develop the next version.

Tags
>   The way you identify a specific version of a file, directory, project, etc.

Merging
>   When two or more developers are working on the same file, the changes must be merged.

Locking
>   How the SCM determines who can make a change to a file. In a pessimistic locking system, only one person at a time can make changes to a file. In an optimistic system, many people can make changes, and all the changes are automatically merged when the file is checked in.

> ### The Cost of a Tool
>
> Many development teams prefer to use free tools, while others prefer commercial products with support contracts. We tend to favor tools that are freely available and get support from the user community, but we don't pick tools based on the cost. We choose tools based on what works.¹ If several tools can fill the need our team has, we'll pick the free one. You'll need to figure out what works in your environment.

How to Choose:

Features

> Tags—Is it easy to tag specific versions of your source code? Is it easy to use tags to access that code?
>
> Merging—Are your merges manual or automatic?
>
> Multiproject projects—Can you include other projects, modules, and versions in your project? How hard is it to define interproject dependencies?

Ease of use

> Does the system integrate with the the editors or IDEs your team is using? Can it be embedded within your build scripts? Remember, if it's not convenient to use, nobody will use it.

Scalability

> Can the system handle all your files? Projects? Users? Without losing or corrupting files?

Performance

> Are the basic operations fast enough to be worthwhile, or will people bypass them because they don't want to wait?

For More Information:

See Practice 2, *Manage Assets*, on page 20.

Appendix C

Build Scripting Tools

Scripting languages take a lot of the work out of building your product. With features specific to product compilation and assembly, these languages let you capture every step of your build process so that it's repeatable and easy to automate.

What's Available:

OS Scripting Languages (e.g. Shell, Batch Files)

These are available on your existing operating system, but tend to be very generic and lack many of the common functions you'll need. Use them, and you risk reinventing the wheel.

make

make............................http://sources.redhat.com/cygwin
make comes on all modern Unix and Unix-like systems; you can get a free version for Windows at this URL.

make is the grandaddy of all the build scripts, and has been around for decades. Tools like make move you forward a little, but still force you to write your own code for many common functions. They do begin to introduce the idea of a cross platform script.

Automake...................http://www.gnu.org/software/automake
Automake is a Perl utility that helps you create make files.

Language-Specific Tools

There are a number of tools that have been written for specific languages. For instance, Ant was created for the Java language, and it can create JAR files and WAR files, generate JavaDocs, and so on. Using tools like Ant helps insulate you from the details of creating WAR files while at the same time providing a robust and repeatable way to build your WAR files.

Ant . . . . `http://ant.apache.org`
Ant is the standard build scripting language for Java work. With tons of built-in functionality, it's flexible enough to script much more than just Java.

NAnt . . . . `http://nant.sourceforge.net`
NAnt is the .Net version of Ant.

Groovy . . . . `http://groovy.codehaus.org`
While definitely a general scripting language, Groovy also lets you access all the functionality of Ant from within your Java code. Its goal is to give you all the convenience of Ant targets with the power of a real programming language as well. Groovy is still maturing, so *caveat emptor*.

Rake . . . . `http://rake.rubyforge.org/`
Rake is a build tool for Ruby with similar capabilities to make, but it uses pure Ruby for its scripting language. It also supports such things as rules patterns and tasks with prerequisites.

General Scripting Languages

Strictly speaking, scripting languages were not intended for build systems, but since many people already know one and then get asked to create a build system, often general-purpose scripting languages get pressed into action. To be blunt, we've never seen a good build system based on a general-purpose language. We're including this section for completeness, but we encourage you strongly to use a tool specifically designed for the job.

Ruby . . . . `http://www.ruby-lang.org/`
Ruby is a scripted language that's getting more popular every day. It has many object-oriented features built in and can process text files like Perl. It's easy to use, is very clean, and has an active user community.

Python . . . . `http://www.python.org/`
Python is another interpreted language with many object-oriented features. People either love or hate Python's format, but it's hard to ignore the fervor that hard-core fans have for it.

Perl . . . . `http://www.perl.org/`
No discussion of scripting languages would be complete without mentioning Perl. Perl has been around for years, exists on every major platform, and has been used to do nearly everything a computer can do. It's got an incredibly rich

set of functionality for handling text files, and the web archives[1] have Perl code available to do anything you'll ever need done. The syntax is obscure, but the utility is undeniable.

Build Systems

Maven. . . . . `http://maven.apache.org`
Tools like Maven move you one step higher on the food chain. The main complaint with this category is that they encapsulate too much. Maven has very specific preferences about build locations and task names, but you can work around them. Most people seem to either love or hate this type of tool. Try it for yourself!

Maven 2. . . . . `http://maven.apache.org/maven2/index.html`
The next version of Maven, rewritten from the ground up. The build paradigm is simpler than in Maven 1, and performance has been greatly enhanced.

Key Concepts:

Syntax
> The tool's language. make and its kind are pretty arcane, but most late-model scripts are based on XML.

Tasks
> What the tool can actually accomplish. At a minumum you need compile and linking features, but tools like Ant do a lot more.

Script interpreter
> The "engine" that executes your script.

How to Choose:

Comprehensive
> Can you do everything you need without writing a lot of custom code?

Readable
> Can anyone in your shop read the script and understand it?

Available on your platform
> Is it ubiquitous?

---

[1]`http://cpan.perl.org`

Scalable

Is it fast enough? Can it handle the load needed in your shop? There's a big difference in being able to handle one or two projects and handling fifty.

Extensible

How hard is it going to be for you to add those extra functions you need?

Flexible

Can you use the tool the way you want to, or will the tool force you to change the way you work?

Matches your programming style

Just because it works doesn't mean it's the best fit for you!

Easily accomplishes your build tasks

Can you learn it in thirty minutes, or will it take two weeks?

For More Information:

See Practice 3, *Script Your Build*, on page 26.

Continuous Integration Systems

A CI system automatically builds your project every time you make a change to it. It watches some set of resources (such as a source code repository, a file system, or even another project), and when they change, it kicks off your build script. When the build is complete, the CI system tells you (or any other important party) the results of the build.

What's Available:

CruiseControl .... `http://cruisecontrol.sourceforge.net`
An open-source CI system written in Java, CruiseControl has a lot of functionality and an active developer base. It's the one we use.

CruiseControl.NET .... `http://sourceforge.net/projects/ccnet`
CruiseControl for the .NET Framework. A somewhat different set of features than CC for Java but the same concept.

AntHill .... `http://www.urbancode.com/projects/anthill`
Termed a *build management server*, AntHill imposes its own build scheme on the build process. However, it has a very nice web interface instead of configuration files. This makes setting up your projects almost trivial. AntHill has both an open-source and commercial version, with extra features available only in the commercial version.

Continuum .... `http://maven.apache.org/continuum`
Continuum is a new CI system that is designed to be very tightly integrated with Maven. It has a "zero configuration" feature that will seamlessly integrate an existing Maven project.

Key Concepts:

Configuration
> How you set up the system. A lot of CI systems use configuration files, but some (e.g., AntHill) use a web-based interface.

CI "engine"
> What actually watches for changes and executes the builds.

External interfaces (e.g., JMX, RMI, web page, COM, XML-RPC)
> How you control the CI system while it's running.

Supported build tools
> The things that the CI system can do (e.g., compiling, linking, deploying, installing).

Integration with other tools
> Running new tools from your CI system.

Notification mechanisms
> Ways to notify the CI system's users that a build succeeded or failed. This can include email, web pages, RSS feeds, or lava lamps.

Logging and metering
> Tracking and presenting information about what got built when and whether the build passed or failed.

How to Choose:

Can easily build your project
> Can the CI system build your project without jumping through a lot of configuration hoops?

Runs on your platform
> Does it run everywhere you need it?

Works with your other tools
> Can you easily tie in your code profiler, installer, deployment tool, etc.?

Scales to the number of projects you need to build
> If you have a lot of projects to build, you need a speedy CI system.

Fully automatic
> No manual steps should be required.

Provides appropriate notification
  Can it tell you what's going on in a way you'll notice?

For More Information:

See Practice 4, *Build Automatically*, on page 31.

There is an excellent feature matrix on the web.[1]

---

[1] http://docs.codehaus.org/display/DAMAGECONTROL/
Continuous+Integration+Server+Feature+Matrix

Issue Tracking Software

Issue tracking software manages your projects' lists of bugs, things to do, and other items of interest. Properly used, these lists become the "memory" for your project.

What's Available:

Bugzilla . . . . `http://www.bugzilla.org`
An open-source web-based bug tracking system. Bugzilla is widely used by many organizations including Mozilla and Red Hat.

FogBugz . . . . `http://www.fogcreek.com/FogBugz`
Another commercial product from Fog Creek Software, the company of Joel Spolsky (of "Joel on Software" fame).

JIRA . . . . `http://www.atlassian.com/software/jira/default.jsp`
"Try-before-buy" system with extensions for such things as email, RSS, Excel, XML, and CVS. This is the system that the CruiseControl project uses.

Trac . . . . `http://projects.edgewall.com/trac`
Trac is an open source project that integrates with Subversion and has a built-in Wiki. It's becoming increasing popular and is worthy of a closer look.

PR-Tracker . . . . `http://www.prtracker.com`
An enterprise-level web-based bug tracking system. Licensing is based on users, not computers.

Key Concepts:

Issue entry

> How you get the details of your issue into the system. Some tools use a web interface to enter the issue descriptions, and others need you to load client software onto your system.

Issue description
> What the issue is and, if appropriate, how to reproduce it.

Assignment
> Who's going to work on it.

Prioritization
> How important the issue is relative to all the other issues in the system.

Search
> Finding relevant issues based on criteria such as product, user, priority, etc.

Reporting
> Generates reports of the issues based on relevant criteria.

Notification
> Notifies the appropriate parties when something in the system changes (new issue, change in issue status, etc.)

Integration with other tools
> Tie-ins with notification systems, source code management systems, report generation tools, etc.

User-specific operations
> Limit operations based on user permissions, and allow customers to file bug reports.

How to Choose:

Interface
> Is it easy to perform the operations you do frequently? Can you get to the system from everywhere you need to?
>
> - Web-based—All you need is a web browser.
>
> - Client-server—You need the client installed on your machine to access the system.
>
> - Local—You can access the system only from a single machine.

Scalable
> Will it handle all your projects and their issues? Can it handle all your users?

Not too complex

    If it's not easy to use, nobody will use it.

Tracks the info you need

    Does the tool capture all the information you care about? Does it require information you don't need?

Generates the reports you need

    Will this tool give you the reports you need out of the box, or will the standard reports require significant customization? Is the information you care about even available?

Notification options

    Such as email, RSS, web pages, wikis, etc.

Supports/integrates with your existing tools

    Otherwise, you'll have to move information back and forth manually.

Runs on your platforms

    If you have developers working on multiple platforms (PC, Mac, Unix, etc.) make sure they all have access to the tool.

For More Information:

See Practice 5, *Track Issues*, on page 36 and Practice 6, *Track Features*, on page 40.

Development Methodologies

It sometimes seems as if there are as many different ways to develop software as there are developers. New ones appear all the time. Keep up-to-date with the thought leaders in the field, see what they come up with, and try it in your own shop.

One methodology to avoid: the infamous Waterfall method. This has been universally discredited in more forward-looking development circles, but it's amazing how many shops still use it. The Waterfall model assumes that you can compeletely understand every phase of your project and set a concrete schedule for each phase. The Waterfall method also expects you to set this schedule before you've even started the project! Clueless managers who like schedules have been fans of the Waterfall for years.

What's Available:

Tracer Bullet Development . . . . www.PragmaticProgrammer.com
This is the methodology we use, and we're rather partial to it! See Section 4, *Tracer Bullet Development*, on page 105.

Agile Development . . . . http://www.agilealliance.com/home
More a movement than a specific methodology, it emphasizes adaptability, communication, and iteration.

Capability Maturity Model: (CMM, SW-CMM, or CMMI). . .
. . . http://www.sei.cmu.edu/cmmi
Formal models for most facets of the software development process.

eXtreme Programming (XP) . . . . http://www.extremeprogramming.org
Developed by Kent Beck, XP's rules and practices include pair programming, iterations, and lots of customer interaction.

Rational Unified Process (RUP)...

...`http://www-136.ibm.com/developerworks/rational/products/rup`
A large, formal methodology with many different facets.

Scrum...................................`http://www.controlchaos.com`
An agile methodology that organizes around incremental delivery cycles called *sprints*.

Crystal .... `http://alistair.cockburn.us/crystal/crystal.html`
Crystal is a highly adaptive software process. It's based on the idea that every project is different, so every project will need a different methodology.

Key Concepts:

Phases

> The series of steps you take throughout the course of your project. Different methodologies have different phases, but most include phases such as requirements gathering, coding, testing, and writing documentation.

Milestones

> Specific events that occur or items you deliver during development.

Deliverables

> Pieces of software that go "out the door" to interested parties (e.g., code, documentation, demos).

Schedule

> When the milestones must be accomplished.

Work assignments

> The members of the team are assigned specific tasks, and completion of those tasks is tracked.

Communication

> Nobody on the team is allowed to work in a vacuum.

How to Choose:

Type of product

> What software are you developing? A small project needs a different sort of methodology than a big one.

Size of the team
> A small team can be successful with a less formal methodology than a large one.

Type of people on the team
> Some people work better with less formality, supervision, and planning than others.

Type of customer
> Your customer might or might not be available for consultation during the project.

External constraints
> Sometimes you'll be required to use a certain methodology (e.g., contractual, government auditing).

Past record
> If your current methodology ain't broke, don't fix it!

Simplicity
> Large, complex methodologies might be more than a small team can handle.

For More Information:

See Section 4, *Tracer Bullet Development*, on page 105.

Martin Fowler's article on methodologies has a great discussion of this topic at `martinfowler.com/articles/newMethodology.html`.

Testing Frameworks

A testing framework gives you a place to organize and run your tests without worrying about the low-level plumbing. We talk about two kinds here: tests harnesses and test tools. A *test harness* is an API that you can use as the basis for writing your own tests. A *test tool* is a program that you use to create and run tests. Both have their place, depending on what you're testing.

What's Available (Test Harnesses):

SUnit .... http://sunit.sourceforge.net
SmallTalk Unit is the original XUnit testing harness. This is the one that all the current unit testing frameworks copied.

JUnit .... http://www.junit.org
One of the more popular testing frameworks, written in Java for Java.

JUnitPerf ...... http://www.clarkware.com/software/JUnitPerf.html
A nice collection of JUnit extensions that make performance and scalability measurement easier. This is a great example of why you want to use an open tool. Lots of people extend open tools, and the extensions are the sort of thing you'd have to write for yourself if you used a toolkit you wrote.

NUnit .... http://www.nunit.org
A unit testing harness for .NET, originally ported from JUnit. It supports all the .NET languages.

MbUnit .... http://www.mbunit.org
Built on top of NUnit, MbUnit brings several higher-level testing techniques to the table. Integrated combinatorial testing, reporting, row testing, data-driven testing, and other concepts are all part of the package.

HTMLUnit . . . . `http://htmlunit.sourceforge.net`
Used inside another test harness (such as JUnit), HTMLUnit simulates a web browser to test web applications.

HTTPUnit . . . . `http://httpunit.sourceforge.net`
HTTPUnit is a lot like HTMLUnit, but it uses HTTP requests and responses to do its testing.

JWebUnit . . . . `http://jwebunit.sourceforge.net`
JWebUnit sits on top of HTTPUnit to give you a high-level API for navigating a web app.

What's Available (Testing Tools):

Cobertura . . . . `http://cobertura.sourceforge.net`
Cobertura (Spanish for "coverage") is a code coverage tool. When you run a set of tests, it tells you how much tests exercise the tested code.

Clover . . . . `http://www.cenqua.com/clover`
Another code coverage tool, Clover has integrated plug-ins for most of the popular IDEs out there.

Fit . . . . `http://fit.c2.com`
Fit takes a unique, user-friendly, table-driven approach to acceptance tests. It's worth reading about even if you choose not to use it.

Fitnesse . . . . `http://fitnesse.org`
An extension to Fit. Fitnesse is both a stand-alone wiki and an acceptance testing framework.

WinRunner . . . . `http://www.mercury.com`
Winrunner is an enterprise-class tool for functional and regression testing (and has a price tag to match).

LoadRunner . . . . `http://www.mercury.com`
From the same company as WinRunner, LoadRunner handles performance and stress testing.

Empirix E-Tester . . . . `http://www.empirix.com`
Empirix is a web recorder/playback tool that embeds MS Internet Explorer.

Watir . . . . `http://wtr.rubyforge.org`
A testing tool to drive automated tests inside Internet Explorer. By driving IE, it solves the problem of imitating a specific browser's interpretation of a web page. It's based on Ruby and is becoming more popular.

Systir . . . . `http://atomicobject.com/systir.page`
Another Ruby-based tool. This one is designed to drive tests in other languages.

Key Concepts:

API

> The programmatic interface that your test code uses to access the test harness.

Methodology for creating tests

> The framework that the test harness exposes.

User Interface

> How you create, save, run, and maintain tests.

Test engine

> The program that actually runs the tests you create.

Results display

> How you find out whether the tests passed or failed.

How to Choose:

Type of testing

> Does the tool or harness let you run the tests you need (e.g., functional, performance)?

Support for the stuff you're testing

> Does the tool let you test your application code? Your web site?

Supported programming languages

> Can you test the languages you use natively, or do you have to learn a new technology?

Flexibility

> Can you create and run the type of tests that you need for your program?

Open formats

> Can you integrate your test tool with other tools?

For More Information:

See Practice 7, *Use a Testing Harness*, on page 43.

For an extensive list of testing frameworks, visit these web sites.

- `http://www.xprogramming.com/software.htm`
- `http://www.testingfaqs.org/t-unit.html`

Appendix H

Suggested Reading List

Some of these books we've read ourselves, and some were suggested by reviewers. Read over the list, and try to pick out a title or two you haven't read yet.

General

The Pragmatic Programmer by Andy Hunt and Dave Thomas. This book is a classic text on personal practices. It should be a desktop reference for everyone who writes code for a living.

Mastering Regular Expressions by Jeffrey Friedl. Regular expressions are the most powerful way to process text we've ever come across, but the "Here Be Dragons" factor is extremely high. This book handily slays the little beasties.

The Mythical Man-Month by Frederick Brooks. Will realized after reading this book (the first edition, in college no less!) how much more there is to software development than simply coding up a program.

The Art of Computer Programming by Donald Knuth. There are multiple volumes in this set. They are a comprehensive introduction to classical computer science.

Death March: The Complete Software Developer's Guide to Surviving "Mission Impossible" Projects by Edward Youdon. Death March projects are famous in the software industry. Understand them so you don't get swept along by them.

Refactoring: Improving the Design of Existing Code by Martin Fowler. A great introduction to the ideas behind refactoring as well as lots of practical suggestions.

Refactoring to Patterns by Joshua Kerievsky. You've read about patterns, and you've read about refactoring. Now see the various patterns in refactoring projects.

Enterprise Integration Patterns by Hophe and Woolf. This book is to distributed and N-tier systems what *Design Patterns* is to an individual program. Again, let someone else point out common pitfalls and solutions. Just reading this book will give you some great ideas for your next project.

Working Effectively with Legacy Code by Michael Feather. This book is a practical guide for testing, refactoring, and extending the product you inherited.

Code Complete by Steve McConnell. A well-known collection of best practices in building software.

Ruby

Programming Ruby by David Thomas with Chad Fowler and Andy Hunt. The book on Ruby for us non-Japanese speakers. Gives you everything you need to know to get a handle on the language.

The Ruby Way by Hal Fulton. Takes up where *Programming Ruby* leaves off. Saves you an immense amount of time figuring out how to best use the language for common tasks.

Java

Java Network Programming by Merlin Hughes et. al. This book taught us how to write networking code. Period. Nuff said. (The Java part was an extra added bonus.)

Pragmatic Project Automation by Mike Clark. A complete guide to setting up and automating your projects infrastructure. A great read for developers of any language!

Pragmatic Unit Testing in Java by Andy Hunt and Dave Thomas. A great guide to getting started with JUnit (there's a version for C# and .NET as well).

Methodologies

Test Driven Development by Kent Beck. As much about design as testing, this one turned our ideas about program design and implementation on their heads.

Crystal Clear: A Human-Powered Methodology for Small Teams by Allistair Cockburn. Crystal is a popular agile methodology

Extreme Programming Explained: Embrace Change by Kent Beck. Interested in XP? Then you should read this book.

Extreme Programming Applied: Playing to Win by Ken Auer. Widely considered the most practical of all the XP texts, it's another must read for anyone using XP.

Agile Software Development with Scrum by Ken Schwaber and Mike Beedle. Scrum is a great lightweight methodology. The name comes from rugby.

Source Code Management

Pragmatic Version Control Using CVS by Dave Thomas and Andy Hunt. Although we had used CVS for years, we found we didn't know as much about it as we thought we did. Answered questions we didn't even know we had.

Pragmatic Version Control Using Subversion by Mike Mason. Required reading for anyone learning Subversion.

Miscellaneous

The Little Schemer by Daniel Friedman and Matthias Felleisen. Opened our eyes to a whole new way of looking at programs, algorithms, and recursion. Talk about thinking outside the mainstream development box!

Dynamic HTML: The Definitive Reference by Danny Goodman. Our bible during a long, LONG summer of cross-browser web development. For almost every problem we ran into, this book had an explanation and more often than not, a solution.

Bugs in Writing: A Guide to Debugging Your Prose by Lyn Dupre. If you ever plan to write anything, read this book before you start, not while you write (like we did!). Lyn's funny and effective advice will help you turn your ideas into readable books, articles, and reports.

UML Distilled by Martin Fowler. You don't have to use UML to benefit from this book. It's a great introduction the Unified Modeling Language (UML) and how to visually represent your software.

Leadership and People

21 Irrefutable Laws of Leadership by John Maxwell. Like the law of gravity, you can either learn the laws or break yourself against them. This book is an invaluable insight into how people lead (or should lead).

Seven Habits of Highly Effective People by Stephen Covey. This book explains clearly how to organize your life–and why you should bother! It's essential reading for anyone who wants to be effective at home or work.

Peopleware: Product Projects and Teams by DeMarco and Lister. A classic text, this book talks about common problems teams encounter and how to avoid them. Additionally, it will show you some key concepts your team can use to succeed where so many others have failed.

How to Win Friends and Influence People by Dale Carnegie. This book is the definitive guide to successful relationships (both personal and professional). This book has sold more than 15 million copies for good reason. If you haven't read it, you owe it to yourself.

H.1 Bibliography

[Cla04]   Mike Clark. *Pragmatic Project Automation. How to Build, Deploy, and Monitor Java Applications.* The Pragmatic Programmers, LLC, Raleigh, NC, and Dallas, TX, 2004.

[Coc01]   Alistair Cockburn. *Agile Software Development.* Addison Wesley Longman, Reading, MA, 2001.

[Cus03]   Cusumano. A global survey of software development practices. Technical Report 178, MIT Sloan School of Mgmt, June 2003. `http://ebusiness.mit.edu/research/papers/178_Cusumano_Intl_Comp.pdf`.

[HT00]   Andrew Hunt and David Thomas. *The Pragmatic Program-mer: From Journeyman to Master*. Addison-Wesley, Reading, MA, 2000.

[TH03]   David Thomas and Andrew Hunt. *Pragmatic Version Control Using CVS*. The Pragmatic Programmers, LLC, Raleigh, NC, and Dallas, TX, 2003.

[You99]   Edward Yourdon. *Death March: The Complete Software Developer's Guide to Surviving 'Mission Impossible' Projects*. Prentice Hall, Englewood Cliffs, NJ, 1999.

[Zei01]   Alan Zeichick. Debuggers, source control keys to quality. *Software Development Times*, March 2001.

Index

Pragmatic Starter Kit Series

Version Control. **Unit Testing**. **Project Automation**. Three great titles, one objective. To get you up to speed with the essentials for successful project development. Keep your source under control, your bugs in check, and your process repeatable with these three concise, readable books from the Pragmatic Bookshelf.

• Keep your project assets safe—never lose a great idea • Know how to UNDO bad decisions—no matter when they were made • Learn how to share code safely, and work in parallel • See how to avoid costly code freezes • Manage third-party code • Understand how to go back in time, and work on previous versions.

Pragmatic Version Control Using CVS
Dave Thomas and Andy Hunt
(176 pages) ISBN: 0-9745140-0-4. $29.95

Pragmatic Version Control Using Subversion
Mike Mason
(224 pages) ISBN: 0-9745140-6-3. $29.95

• Write better code, faster • Discover the hiding places where bugs breed • Learn how to think of all the things that could go wrong • Test pieces of code without using the whole project • Use JUnit to simplify your test code • Test effectively with the whole team.

Pragmatic Unit Testing
Andy Hunt and Dave Thomas
(176 pages) ISBN: 0-9745140-1-2. $29.95
(Also available for C#, ISBN: 0-9745140-2-0)

• Common, freely available tools which automate build, test, and release procedures • Effective ways to keep on top of problems • Automate to create better code and save time and money • Create and deploy releases easily and automatically • Have programs to monitor themselves and report problems.

Pragmatic Project Automation
Mike Clark
(176 pages) ISBN: 0-9745140-3-9. $29.95

Visit our secure online store: http://pragmaticprogrammer.com/catalog

Facets of Ruby Series

Learn how to use the popular Ruby programming language from the Pragmatic Programmers: your definitive source for reference and tutorials on the Ruby language and exciting new application development tools based on Ruby.

The *Facets of Ruby* series includes the definitive guide to Ruby, widely known as the PickAxe book. Upcoming titles in this series feature the *Ruby on Rails* web application framework and other exciting new technologies.

• The definitive guide for Ruby programmers. • Up-to-date and expanded for Ruby version 1.8. • Complete documentation of all built-in classes, modules, and methods. • Complete descriptions of all ninety-eight standard libraries. • 200+ pages of new content in this edition. • Learn more about Ruby's web tools, unit testing, and programming philosophy.

Programming Ruby: The Pragmatic Programmer's Guide, 2nd Edition
Dave Thomas with Chad Fowler and Andy Hunt
(864 pages) ISBN: 0-9745140-5-5. $44.95

• Learn all about this new open-source, full-stack web framework. • Develop sophisticated web applications quickly and easily. • Use incremental and iterative development to create the web apps that users want. • Get to go home on time.

Agile Web Development with Rails: A Pragmatic Guide
Dave Thomas and David Heinemeier Hansson
(450 pages) ISBN: 0-9766940-0-X. $34.95

Visit our store at http://pragmaticprogrammer.com/catalog

The Pragmatic Bookshelf

The Pragmatic Bookshelf features books written by developers for developers. The titles continue the well-known Pragmatic Programmer style, and continue to garner awards and rave reviews. As development gets more and more difficult, the Pragmatic Programmers will be there with more titles and products to help programmers stay on top of their game.

Visit Us Online

Ship It!
pragmaticprogrammer.com/titles/prj
Source code from this book, errata, and other resources. Come give us feedback, too!

Register for Updates
pragmaticprogrammer.com/updates
Be notified when updates and new books become available.

Join the Community
pragmaticprogrammer.com/community
Read our weblogs, join our online discussions, participate in our mailing list, interact with our wiki, and benefit from the experience of other Pragmatic Programmers.

New and Noteworthy
pragmaticprogrammer.com/news
Check out the latest pragmatic developments in the news.

Save on the PDF

Save more than 60% on the PDF version of this book. Owning the paper version of this book entitles you to purchase the PDF version for only $7.50 (regularly $20). That's a saving of more than 60%. The PDF is great for carrying around on your laptop. It's hyperlinked, has color, and is fully searchable. Buy it now at pragmaticprogrammer.com/coupon

Contact Us

Phone Orders:	1-800-699-PROG (+1 919 847 3884)
Online Orders:	www.pragmaticprogrammer.com/catalog
Customer Service:	orders@pragmaticprogrammer.com
Non-English Versions:	translations@pragmaticprogrammer.com
Pragmatic Teaching:	academic@pragmaticprogrammer.com
Author Proposals:	proposals@pragmaticprogrammer.com